Praise for Beyond Your Shadows of Doubt

"Prepare yourself for a profound experience of inspiration and healing. Like me, you will know in the first few lines that it is no accident you have been guided to this beautiful book, written by a courageous author. The world has been waiting for these words. It will change lives in all the best ways."

—Jan Stringer, founder PerfectCustomers, Inc.
Author of *Bee-ing Attraction, Attracting Perfect Customers*
http://www.perfectcustomers.com

"Judy's life has brought forth this wonderful book to the universe, and what a pilgrimage for its lucky readers to share in the great discovery of what qualities a champion is made of.

"This book indeed is a gift to the world, a gift filled with the real-life experiences of the author, whom I have had the honor and privilege of knowing in this lifetime.

"Judy K. Katz has taken the full spectrum of her life experiences, from the heights of financial success to the depths of despair, out of which she has emerged as the observer of her own struggle for meaning, and finding that meaning, she wisely has turned it into the ultimate source of happiness by transforming meaning into bliss.

"This is the kind of writing that leads to an awakening of the most profound kind: discovery of the power of love in the midst of darkest hours, giving one the courage to release what no longer works, and the energy that can propel you into prosperity, success, and the joy of life.

"***Beyond Your Shadows of Doubt: Ascend Out of Fear and Conflict into Confidence and Authentic Power*** is a must-read if you want to go beyond limits, discover your purpose, and live the life of your highest dreams."

—Reverend H. Patrick Pollard, RSc.F
Founding spiritual leader Connecticut Center for Spiritual Living
http://www.ctcsl.org/

"With Judy, I have learned to recognize what really matters and to become aware of exciting possibilities. I am consciously living for the first time. Today I am writing a new story from this place. I'm living a truly abundant life.

"I have learned to trust, to communicate more genuinely, to listen with all that I have and to enrich my overall way of 'being in the world.' I honestly believe now that anything is possible. Believe me, Judy is an absolute gem who can support you through your most difficult moments and will take life from ordinary to extraordinary.

"I am so truly grateful for Judy's work with me. She has touched my soul and has touched my spirit. This has allowed me to travel back to myself and build the most wonderful relationship with the self inside of me that yearns to be cared for and loved.

"I often say to my dearest friends, the relationship that takes the most work is the one wherein we fall deeply back into love with our self. One in which we cherish all the remarkable shadows and habits that have protected us for so, so long.

"Judy K. Katz is my mentor, my coach, my friend, the nurturing touch, the one that gets me, the me in you, the you in me. What words can I ever find to express the gratitude and the joy that her work has brought back into my being."

—Nancy LaSalle
http://www.accessoneleadership.com
Calgary, AB, Canada

"I would have to write a book to explain all of the ways that Judy has helped me to change my life. The changes have been deep and profound and I am forever changed … this is not temporary and it can't be unlearned.

"As I have come to understand, we hold a mask of self-deception that won't allow us to see the very techniques we use to hold ourselves apart from all of the good that we deserve. This self-deception shows up in a lot of the strategies that we use to help us cope with life. We need someone outside of ourselves to shine the light on those strategies and uncover them, which allows us to use our Higher Power so that we are open to receive the ease and flow that is available to us.

"Judy describes this like losing your keys on the ground, and you're scrambling around in the dark trying to find them. Then someone turns on a streetlamp that illuminates the ground and you can instantly find your keys. I would describe her as one of those huge megawatt lights that they use to help you find the parking lot of a Rolling Stones concert!

"Through my work with Judy, we have ferreted out the energies that run me and keep me contracted in my personal and professional life. I have realized that most of my actions were taken from a place of fear and were put in place to keep me 'safe.' That pattern had such a strong hold on me. It was quite clearly the reason why no matter how hard I tried or how many new ways I would do something, the result was always the same. I felt hopeless and very defeated.

"Judy has helped me to recognize the pattern, taught me how to break the habit and how to use a different energy to expand my life instead of holding myself back in fear and contraction."

—Mardi Lo Faso, president Community Based Marketing, Inc.
http://www.communitybasedmarketing.com

BEYOND YOUR SHADOWS OF DOUBT

ASCEND OUT OF FEAR AND CONFLICT
INTO CONFIDENCE AND AUTHENTIC POWER

— by Judy K. Katz —

Copyright © 2013 Judy K. Katz

ALL RIGHTS RESERVED

No part of this book may be translated, used, or reproduced in any form or by any means, in whole or in part, electronic or mechanical, including photocopying, recording, taping, or by any information storage or retrieval system without the express written permission from the author or the publisher except for the use in brief quotations within critical articles and reviews.

judy@judykkatz.com
www.beyondyourshadowsofdoubt.com

Limits of Liability and Disclaimer of Warranty:
The author and/or publisher shall not be liable for your misuse of this material. The contents are strictly for informational and educational purposes only.

Warning – Disclaimer:
The author of this book does not dispense medical advice or prescribe the use of any technique as a form of treatment for physical, emotional, or medical problems. The intent of the author is to offer information of a general nature to help you in your quest for personal, emotional, and spiritual growth, and for the expansion into higher consciousness.

In the event you use any of the information in this book for yourself, the author and/or the publisher assume no responsibility for your actions or your outcomes. The author and/or publisher shall have neither liability nor responsibility with respect to any loss or damage caused, or alleged to be caused, directly or indirectly, by the information contained in this book.

Printed and bound in the United States of America

ISBN: 13: 978-0615908465
(Beyond Your Shadows of Doubt)
ISBN: 10: 0615908462

Dedication

To my two beautiful daughters, Sheri and Lori,
who gave me the will to never give up
in times when it would have been easier to.

And to my husband Arny, the love of my life,
who has unconditionally loved and encouraged me
to fulfill my life's purpose by doing the work I love.

Acknowledgments

Writing this book took courage beyond anything I have ever known. I am deeply grateful and appreciative for the following people who never let me give up on my dream, even though it took me 18 years to finally bring it out into the world. These people have taught me how to receive unconditional love and support, and I am deeply grateful.

To my dearest soul sister, Bev Williams, who has walked this journey with me long before I realized it was a spiritual journey. I am inspired by her amazing capacity to give unconditional love and support. We have spent tens of thousands of hours over many years in tears and in laughter learning how to live life on purpose and intentionally.

To Carol Courcy and Barb Eisele, my special friends and mastermind partners, for their trust and confidence in me and for their support and encouragement to live from my authentic self and to share my story.

To my brilliant creative director and book project manager, Bethany Kelly, owner of Courageous Creatives, and her amazing team, Frank Steele, editor, Yoko Matsuoka, cover illustrator, and Stefan Merour, designer, whose encouragement and expertise made this book a beautiful reality.

To all of my clients and students over a span of two decades who have given me the privilege to "see" into their souls and to help them have their personal Alchemy of the Shadow experience and shine!

To the many teachers, authors, and spiritual advisers who have shared their wisdom and love with me, who have fueled my passion and desire to never stop learning and growing because of their examples of what is possible.

To my family of origin, who have given me the opportunity to discover what is possible as a result of the power of unconditional love and forgiveness and to experience the miracles of healing as a result.

And finally, to God, the Creator of all that is, the divine spirit of unconditional love, creative power, and infinite possibilities, I am deeply grateful for blessing us all with everything we need to live life joyously, fully, passionately, and intentionally.

Foreword

I met Judy while she was hosting a Robert Panté Dressing to Win seminar. A mutual friend, Michael, insisted that we meet. If you are lucky in life, you will be introduced to a friend like Judy, someone you meet for the first time and instantly recognize, knowing that you've been friends forever. She is my soul sister. Thank you, Michael.

At the time, I had discovered Anthony Robbins' work and, shortly thereafter, entered into a franchise agreement with Anthony Robbins and Associates for the purpose of locally marketing and facilitating Tony's video-based seminars. With our mutual interests in personal/professional/spiritual development, Judy was an ever-present source of support and inspiration for my work.

With a few exceptions, due to moves you will read about in this book, Judy and I have met at least once a week for lunch to share our latest distinctions (aha moments) gleaned from life and study, about the Law of Attraction. I remember very clearly two such distinctions which Judy brought to our table that were turning points in her (and my) life. The first was that the trick to creating a great life is to NOT be at the effect of our circumstances, but rather to understand that they are just a mirror, feedback, reflecting our subconscious patterns. Secondly, she recognized that the missing link to manifesting anything was giving up resistance—resistance to the way things are or were, and even our resistance to our resistance. These insights transformed the shadows of her past into the light of her present.

In this book you will travel with her through a maze of confusion, decisions, mistakes, and retakes she experienced while searching for a way to ascend out of the depths of her despair and create the life of her dreams. On that journey she received the spiritual guidance and clarity needed to define her "Alchemy of the Shadow" process, a process that transformed her life and the lives of clients she has now touched all over the world.

Upon reflection, it's curious to note that when I met Judy in 1988, she was hosting that Panté seminar about not only "looking good" but also about realizing who you really are. These two themes are the alpha and omega of her journey beyond her "shadows of doubt."

As you traverse the pages of this book, may Judy's insights and processes provide the means for you to ascend from fear into your authentic power. I know that was her intent in writing this book.

Bev Williams

CONTENTS

Preface 1
Introduction 5

PART I

My Story of Transformation

Chapter 1	The Great Fall..11
Chapter 2	My Angel Appears...21
Chapter 3	The Power in Forgiveness and Acceptance...........27
Chapter 4	The "Magic" Reappears 47
Chapter 5	My Journey into the Depths of Contrast...............57
Chapter 6	My Feelings—My Powerful Pals 69
Chapter 7	All Things Are Possible................................75
Chapter 8	My Soul Mate—A "Magical" Attraction 83
Chapter 9	The Impossible Dream Comes True.....................91
Chapter 10	Conclusions—Part I 95

PART II

How to Ascend Out of Your Survival System and Miraculously Transform Your Life

Chapter 11	Your Survival System—Fight-Flight-Freeze	101
	Your Oldest Reptilian Brain	102
	God—the Santa Claus Syndrome	105
	Neutral Awareness—Your First Step to Freedom	106
	Distinguishing Your Survival System	107
	The Two Sides of Fear	109
	Resistance—What You Resist Persists!	111
	Your Survival Patterns—Your Body	112
Chapter 12	Contrast—Conflict—Resistance: Oh My!	115
	The Origin of Your Symbiotic Survival Pattern—Fight-and-Flight Twins	117
	Important Keys to Enter into Your Creative Kingdom	119
	The Law of Opposites	121
Chapter 13	Acceptance and Forgiveness—The Golden Keys to Your Kingdom	123
	Acceptance and Forgiveness Allow for Gratitude and Appreciation	126
	Resistance Is the Only Thing that Holds You in Bondage to Your Past	128

| Chapter 14 | Alchemy of the Shadow | 131 |

So let's begin your
"Alchemy of the Shadow" process 133

Your Needs Must Be Met with
Loving and Wiser Means 136

| Chapter 15 | Your Old Tapes Are Exchanged and Transformed ... 137 |

The Observer—You 142

You've Been Given the Gift of Free Will—
Use It Wisely 146

| Chapter 16 | The Great Shift into Love and Power | 147 |

Experience a Quantum Leap Back into
Your Creative Kingdom! 149

Nonresistance Allows for Higher States of
Awareness and Love 150

| Chapter 17 | The Value and Power of "Desire" | 153 |

The Healing Art Within Manifesting
Your Desires 155

Getting Caught in a Sales Trap with Your Desire ... 156

Your Desires Are Not Remedies for Your
Unmet Needs 157

Understanding the Language of Your Desire 158

| Chapter 18 | The Art of Detachment | 165 |

The Truth About Detachment 167

Chapter 19	The Mirror in Your World	169
Chapter 20	Fight or Flight or Your CREATIVE KINGDOM	
	—It's Your Choice	179
	The "Basement" of Your Mind	180
	Ascending to the "Sundeck" of Your Mind	181

Epilogue	187
Recommended Resources	193
About the Author	197

Preface

We live out the stories that we repeatedly tell ourselves and others. By re-creating ourselves as new and powerful characters in our own stories, we are greatly supported and loved by a universe that can only say "yes" to us! Our new stories become true for us, and that is the truth we must come to trust.

You have the power and freedom to re-create yourself and to become a new character in your own new stories. You can become a powerful and loving partner in relationship to all aspects of your life. It is only then that you can choose and experience the stories that you love, stories that are worthy of who you really are! In fact, it is your responsibility and privilege to do so.

This book is intended to help you free yourself from the limited, fearful, and sometimes seemingly powerless characters that you've experienced yourself to be during times of stress, particularly within critical areas of your life, such as your personal relationships, your business or career, your finances and income, and your health.

You will come to know a new you, someone who is capable of experiencing new and wondrous stories that you want to live, stories that are steeped in your heart's desires and passions and that are fueled by the power of unconditional love.

Imagine what it would be like to not live from your childhood survival strategies when you experience challenges and obstacles in the most critical areas of your life. If you've experienced yourself as being small, powerless, or unloved, and you've been driven by your fight-or-flight survival mode in stressful and difficult times, know that your survival behaviors have vigilantly attempted to keep you safe, so that you could be loved, accepted, and powerful. Unfortunately, any actions that you take from your survival realm will leave you feeling unsafe, insecure, powerless, unloved, and unworthy. You get the opposite of your behavior's intention.

Your experiences further validate your beliefs regarding how life is for you. Unquestioned acceptance of these beliefs will bring about results that reflect your beliefs over and over again. Why is this?

You live within a universe of spiritual and mental laws. These laws govern and support life in ways you may not be aware of. You may not know how to fully cooperate with these laws. You may also not fully understand how you are attracting your current circumstances. More importantly, you may not fully know how to attract what you truly want. Often, so many people do not give themselves permission, deep within, to have what is truly meaningful to them. Yet deep longings persist, even in the face of continued disappointment. Could this be you?

The methods that you are taught in order to be, do, or have anything have no power if your feelings of certainty and conviction are not behind them, or at least the intention to become certain and convinced. Also, you may believe in a method or plan to get what you want, but if you feel threatened by your desire, your subconscious beliefs will prevail and they will trump all of the burning desires in your heart.

It is through the "creative process" of life that you will come to know the power that is within you. By learning to work with universal mental and spiritual laws, and by creating an emotional state of mind that supports your desires, you will learn to manifest the truest desires of your heart, easily and effortlessly!

It is my intention to share the transforming experiences that I have encountered with you. Within my story, you will discover how these laws consistently performed for me, whether I was aware of them or not. In Part I of this book, you will see my sacred yet dramatic journey into the depths of my soul. You'll learn what I discovered that transformed my entire life. You will become aware of what brought me out of my "dark night of the soul" and changed everything.

Part II is written with the intent to bring you into deeper levels of awareness and understanding. I guide you through the processes that turned my life around. I also share the vital distinctions that I discovered which allowed me to have the emotional capacity and breakthroughs to do what I needed to do to be released from my survive-or-die way of life.

Introduction

I lived the majority of my early life with my foot stuck on the accelerator of my survival mode, mostly my fear. I thought I was a fearful person at my core. Fear ran so much of my early life. My circumstances in the first half of my life were so threatening to me that I had to shove my fear down deep to survive.

I came to know myself as someone who was driven to succeed and to win. I did win with money and business for a time. However, I also had to face myself as someone who, for the most part, failed miserably in relationships, particularly with men. I had three failed marriages by my late thirties.

I also knew myself as someone who desperately wanted to connect with people in the deepest way without fear running the show and taking me out. I just wasn't able to let myself do that. I wanted connection in the worst way, and I feared it in the greatest way. I actually had a social phobia.

I used to say, "Everything I touch turns to gold, yet why is it that I can be so good in business and so lousy in relationships?" I constantly demanded, "There's just got to be a better way." This was often my mantra well into the wee hours of the night as I paced the hallways in the office building of my escrow company, exhausted and resentful. I was driven to success. I had achieved great financial success, yet because my buttons were stuck on survival autopilot, I felt my life was crazy and out of control. Actually, it was.

Without realizing it, I was living from a place inside of me that believed, "Life is a fight. I'm a loser if I don't win. I just have to win or I'll die." Fortunately, the greater powers knew differently. A greater power of love knew that the truth about me was so much greater than who I had become. Then it happened. I crashed and my BIG crisis became my life for five years! I entered what would become a five-year "dark night of the soul." My journey into the depths of my own personal hell began in 1986.

If you have not had the pleasure of going through such a hell, let me describe mine a bit. I lost everything that I had worked so hard to get. My financial empire had fallen apart and I was alone and terrified. One night, in my small apartment, I took an honest look at my life. I asked myself, "How is it that I've lost everything that is important to me and I can't seem to get any of it back? How can my life be so out of my control in every important area?" I was alone. I had no strength to do anything. I felt completely unplugged from the universe. I was deep into the consequences of living my fight/flight/freeze survival patterns. I had hit bottom.

Food addictions plagued me. I was depressed, alone. I felt betrayed, suicidal, and scared to death. I had nowhere to turn other than inward. I was the only common denominator in all of my horrible, conflicted circumstances. I turned inward and found my salvation through my spiritual path. I found a me that was way beyond my survival reactions of fear. I discovered that I had much more power and love available than I had ever experienced. My life completely turned around.

Introduction

I made a vow that whatever brought me out of the fear-based chaos of my life would have to be so great, I would be compelled to help other people learn how to transcend beyond their fear and anger, discover who they really are, and to know what is possible beyond all of that. I also discovered a better way to make money rather than being driven to work long, hard hours, sacrificing everything that was important to me, like my daughters, and enduring constant stress to prove myself worthy.

I'm sharing my early life because it is an example (a warning) of how a predictable set of difficult circumstances and consequences will continue if you don't pay closer attention to your survival "buttons" when they get pushed. Sooner or later, whether it's through difficult people in your life or painful circumstances, your life will be negatively impacted and you will be called to wake up to yourself, to realize what is really the great truth about yourself, and what is gloriously possible.

That's why I'm writing this book for you. I want to show you how to interrupt the Big Kahuna of all habit patterns: your fight/flight/freeze emotional survival patterns. These patterns breathe scarcity and fear into your life.

Imagine what it would be like if you could live and experience your life from the realm of your true greater self. What if you could confidently live from inspiration and confidence; you could be open and effective in conflicting situations, and you could do the work you're passionate about and be paid extremely well for it? Imagine giving unconditional love to your loved ones and friends, which is what I am quite sure your heart really wants to do.

Your hot buttons are often pushed when a conflict or disturbance occurs in one or more of these areas of your life: your finances, your career, your relationships, and your health. These are, generally speaking, the areas in your life that affect your survival more than any other.

Imagine how much better your life could be if your survival patterns didn't take over. Not to mention what it would be like to feel passion and joy, regardless of what is happening around you; to take conscious control and to create your life the way you want it to be, not be victimized by external circumstances or other people.

I invite you to follow my path to freedom, prosperity, love, and joy. You must, however, begin where you are. If you are stressed out, overworked, and disillusioned, or if you feel unloved and exhausted from trying so hard to achieve perfection to prove that you are good enough, let me shine a light into the dark spaces where you are so that you can be set free to live your life again!

Allow yourself to flow through these pages with hope, and should you feel any of my experiences deep within your heart, you too can be transformed into all of that which you truly desire, even if it doesn't seem possible at the moment.

Dare to dream a bigger dream than ever before. Become the REAL you, someone that YOU are designed to be! Let us begin now!

"If you can dream it and you can own it, then you can make it REAL in your life."

Judy K. Katz

Part I

My Story of Transformation

The Great Fall

It was the spring of 1988, and I decided it was time for me to move back to Santa Fe after having moved away just a little over a year earlier. It felt like it was my safe haven. Santa Fe had been my home for eleven years before everything fell apart in my life. I had a great need for quiet nurturing, as I was just coming out of a very painful divorce. Santa Fe had a very calming effect on me. I needed to curl up into a little ball and roll behind life for a while. Santa Fe was just the place I needed to be.

I found an apartment north of town, an area near where I had lived before everything fell apart. I nestled into 930 square feet of space, which was a shock to my system, since that was the size of my bedroom in the gorgeous home I was thrust out of due to my divorce! Somehow I had myself convinced that this space was terribly cute, and I dressed it with color and class as best I could.

I found myself at the threshold of a new beginning. The only problem was that I was not sure of what. My recent divorce had left me very angry and confused, and my self-esteem had been knocked down many notches. Tied up into that failed dream was also my career in custom home designing and creating. That work inflamed my passions beyond anything I had ever known. I felt so empty inside, and for the first time in my life, I was terrified of a future that looked empty and alone. Each day brought deeper and deeper sorrow, and my only escape from the endless, hopeless mind-play was to read.

I continued with the metaphysical studies that I had embraced years ago. That material validated the personal experiences I had of working with spiritual and mental laws, primarily the Law of Attraction. I had been 100 percent successful in attracting buyers to my premium custom-built homes in 30 days from the time I listed them. I trusted this process because it always worked for me. I had to believe that somehow I could pull myself back into my life if I just practiced what I had learned from my spiritual studies.

Unfortunately, I didn't consciously know what I innately knew. I was struggling to meet the demands that were hurtling toward me faster than I thought I could handle them. I was left with an

IRS debt of $32,000 from the sale of my last custom-built home. Of course, the financial damages of the divorce left nothing to spare, and the income from my escrow business, which I had previously sold, was quickly being consumed. Bankruptcy looked imminent and the loss of a few dear treasures, like my little red Mercedes, pulled at my heartstrings. The level of income I had grown accustomed to as a result of owning my escrow business and of designing, building, and selling my custom homes, looked impossible to regain.

Returning to the workforce to a JOB and being employed by someone else seemed unlikely to alleviate my financial disaster. Never mind the gut-wrenching feelings of humiliation and shame that came from thinking I was a failure. Having to start over, back at what I called "the beginning," was contributing to dragging me down into serious depths of depression and anxiety.

"What am I ever going to do? Where is the God I have come to trust and personally know? Why is everything falling apart?" I routinely pondered questions like these into the wee hours of the night. I was dropping into the deepest, thickest, most empty part of life I could imagine. I felt as though my plug had been pulled from life's source and I was living death.

Thoughts of "checking out of my life" seemed to be the only way I could escape the horror I was experiencing. Fortunately, the precious spirits of my two beautiful daughters transported themselves to me each time I felt like giving up. I would sigh and cry from the depths of my soul, still so confused, "How did all this happen?" I couldn't find the strength to imagine being lifted out of these dark places for very long. After all, I had somehow disconnected myself from God, or so it seemed, because I was so confused and I was receiving no answers. I had no idea what to do.

I did, however, continue delving deeply into my spiritual studies, mainly to escape, as drugs and alcohol didn't seem like a long-term solution to relieve my pain. The disease of alcoholism, which I had perceived plagued my ex-husband, was the target of my anger and the blame for my shattered dreams. I was too angry to turn to drugs for comfort. My reading became an intense, compulsive search for the answers I so desperately needed if I was to continue to exist in my body much longer.

Oddly enough, I prayed to a God who seemed so far away, but I had to believe that someday my persistence would pay off. I needed all the extra help I could get, and, besides, I had nothing to lose. Once again, I gave up. There was nowhere else for me to turn. I had fallen into doubt and despair, although I had said I would never distrust again!

After three months of rigorously reading and praying and reading and praying, I began to reach out to a few very special people who loved me. Although I knew it pained them greatly to see me so lost and distraught, they stood by me and comforted me. They gave me what I was not able to give myself: love and acceptance.

I became a socialite of the personal growth circles. I religiously participated in seminars that revealed my "rackets," better known as my ego defenses. I climbed up and stood on top of telephone poles. I swung down zip lines at mountain retreats, and resorted to immersing myself for six days in San Francisco, traversing high wires 300 feet above the ground, rappelling down mountainsides and running up steep hills until I was nauseous. I was absorbed in my passion to learn everything I could about transformation and creation. I knew if I could just find out what it was that I had tapped into years before that brought me so much financial success before my great fall, I would solve the problems I was now suffering from.

Soon after I came down from the seminar wild rides and the frenzied approach to finding answers that could put my life back together again, I received a call from a friend, Michael, who thought I should meet two interesting people. One was Jim, a man who facilitated fire walking. The second person was Bev Williams, someone who, unbeknownst to me at the time, would turn out to be my true soul sister. Bev was affiliated with Anthony Robbins and Associates. I had just finished reading Robbins' book, *Unlimited Power*. He writes of the powers we have within our minds and how we can change our lives by altering our beliefs. I particularly recall his example of fire walking, and I remembered thinking at the time, "I would never do that!"

Well, by November of that same year, I found myself standing in a circle of thirty people or so, building what seemed to be the largest campfire I had ever seen. The heat of the fire inflamed my face as the cold air of the Sandia Mountains pierced my body. "Have I lost my mind, or will this truly be an opportunity to finally get back in touch with a power I discovered years ago?" I wondered.

We were carefully instructed how to appropriately and successfully walk barefoot on the 1900°F coals. We were told this was going to be perhaps the most profound demonstration of the power of belief, and that we would alter our current belief that fire burns when you touch it! I had been climbing and swinging from heights I never thought possible; however, I had safety gear protecting me each time. "Where are the safety devices for this experience?" I wondered. All I could imagine was altering my feet for a lifetime! I didn't even know what sort of protection there could be.

The truth is, protection is what I wanted to know existed for me, and by safely walking on fire, perhaps I could prove it did. I needed to know that I was loved and protected by a power that was greater than me, and that it was still in my life somewhere.

Jim's lecture beforehand explicitly emphasized the necessity of learning to hear our inner guidance responding to the question, "Am I now ready to walk on the coals?" This was no time to question how close my relationship was to God, for I had never been so intensely committed to listening and trusting in an invisible protection as I was then!

I knew, somehow, that this would bring me back to trusting and believing that I was still connected to the incredible source I had come to know during the period of my success just a few years before. The chill of the night did not affect my body as I stood in the circle surrounding the enormous fire, which was blazing and crackling as the heat grew more intense. It was as if the fire spoke to us, invited our courage, yet seemed to understand our terror and confusion. We harmonized with an "om" sound as the fire tenders raked out the fire into a flat bed of red-hot, glistening, glowing coals. My knees knocked to the rhythm of my body shaking as I thought, "Judy, you don't have to do this if you're too afraid!"

I took deep breaths and remembered why I wanted to walk on the fire. I had to know, once again, that I was truly connected to my God source energy. Walking safely across the coals would let me know that God is still with me and that I'm protected in a way I can always trust. I'll never doubt again! Then, it happened. Someone walked across the coals right before my eyes! I gasped. I felt my heart pounding in my chest as I watched. Another walked . . . and then another. The pressure built. "Oh no, I might be the only one who doesn't walk tonight," I thought. Well, this was no time to think that I had to be like everyone else!

Jim told us we would be transformed just by being in the presence of others walking, but I had to know that God-power was alive in me! More and more people continued to leave their place in the circle, go to the threshold of the fire, and walk. I heard myself repeating the chant we were to say to ourselves as we walked across the fire, "Cool moss, cool moss, cool moss." I stared at the fire. With my heart beating rapidly and my knees shaking, I asked myself, "Am I ready to walk?" My legs turned to putty and my feet froze in place. I was not moving from my spot! My body was frozen. I was petrified!

I took another deep breath and released the hand of the person next to me. Now he approached the coals, waited a moment, and proceeded to walk. My face was flushed and hot, not only from the intense heat of the fire, but also from the heat of the fear of walking across the fire! Then Jim announced, "We have three minutes left. If anyone would still like to walk and their guidance says yes, please proceed now." I took another deep breath.

"Oh, God, I really want to do this," I thought. "I can walk." I felt my body trembling, my heart still pounding out of my chest. I asked again, "Am I ready to walk?" Aware of my trembling body and staring at the coals, I remained steadfast with my intent to walk that night. It seemed like forever, until suddenly a stillness and a peace swept over my entire body, and I found myself moving out of the circle toward the threshold of the fire. My legs were calm and sure, and, as I stood in front of the fire, I felt all the power in the universe moving through me, washing my temples with peace and calm as I directed my focus on thoughts of "cool moss." My heart was calm with peace. I knew I was safe to walk.

I stepped onto the coals concentrating on "cool moss, cool moss, cool moss." I steadied myself as my feet sank into the bed of coals, crunching with each step I took, as if I were stepping on little mounds of popcorn across the ten-foot bed of coals. I sensed warmth beneath my feet as I focused on "cool moss" more intently than I ever thought I could. I reached the other side, looked up and reached for the stars with such elation, and thought, "I wonder if I am burned." I chuckled. "If I have to ask or wonder whether I am burned, how bad can it be?"

We completed the fire walk by quietly returning inside the building where our initial lecture was given to celebrate the experience, not only of walking on the coals, but of discovering our inner guidance. I looked at my feet in total awe and almost disbelief. I didn't have one burn spot on my feet, not anywhere! My brain was trying to catch up with the fact that I could walk on fire and not be burned.

Perhaps this experience would allow me to never again need to doubt my connection to a God of power and love. This was truly an experience of an inner power beyond human comprehension or explanation, although some try to explain it. I didn't recognize what I was feeling; it was disorienting for a few moments. I realized that I was protected every inch of the way and did not get burned. "God is still with me." I sighed with relief.

My Angel Appears

It became apparent to me that the time had come for me to leave Santa Fe and move closer to my precious daughters in Albuquerque. Part of the emptiness and needlessness I felt came from the fact that my role as their mother had changed. My reasons for existing also had to change. All I had ever been was a wife, mother, and businesswoman. I had no sense of my own importance beyond my roles. The pain of my previously failed marriage was easing. The idea of creating the relationship of my dreams seemed more of a possibility now. I was clearer than ever before about what

I wanted. It was time to slip out of the shell I had climbed into in Santa Fe and begin to participate in life once again.

Soon after my move back to Albuquerque, I became involved with David. He claimed to be as eager to figure out life as I was. Our survival habits of steering away from the painful experiences of our past and living in denial of them remained concealed from us both, in spite of our diligent commitments to growth. We were on and off for a tormenting year. It was puzzling to me how I could have been so off base when I thought I knew just what I wanted; however, I ended up with exactly what I did not want. How did this happen again?

I managed to fall into a freelance design project for the home I had designed and sold, the year before. This carried me to the end of the year, which brought me to the end of my relationship with David and the end of my rope once again.

With my energy level so low and feeling that familiar loss I had suffered two years earlier with my divorce, I moved in with my youngest daughter, Lori. I held high hopes that I would still find the answers I was searching for regarding my career and my ever-increasing desire to have the relationship of my dreams. I sold the remains of my jewelry and furniture just to get by, as the design project which had carried me for so long was complete. The IRS debt was heavy, increasing steadily, and looming in my mind constantly. My resistance to the fact that I might have to return to the workforce for a third of the income I had enjoyed while self-employed became more intense. The humiliation and embarrassment of my lifestyle caused me to decide, "I don't care about my 'stuff' anymore." I decided that I'd rather seek a spiritual path and transcend my material desires. That seemed to relieve some of the pain and concern of not having more in my life.

My financial situation loomed over me like a huge, dark cloud. I was bankrupt. My little red Mercedes and all my treasured possessions were gone. Thank God, Lori had enough to furnish our apartment. My spiritual studies and my insatiable quest for answers increased; my searching became intense. I decided to write down all that I wanted in detail. I noted the date by which I wanted to receive each desire that I had, particularly in the area of relationships, money, and my career.

Somehow, I felt like a child asking for a new bicycle from Santa year after year after year, only to end up so disappointed that eventually I just wanted to give up and resign myself to living with the restlessness. I felt incomplete and completely ignored.

I found peace in meditating more frequently during this frustrating time. During many of my meditations, I had recurring visions of a beautiful garden with a "little me" sitting beneath the trees on a bench, visiting with a very Beautiful Being who looked like a Cinderella or a Fairy Godmother. I could sense her love and understanding, thus the little me felt very special and safe.

Time melted away as I watched and sensed the love between these two, when suddenly, during a lengthy meditation one day, this Beautiful Being who I lovingly gazed on in my mind's eye turned and looked straight at me! Her face came closer. Her eyes pierced my soul with an intensity that felt like an electric shock to my heart. I gasped, jumped out of my skin, and thought, "I didn't make that figure turn and look at me! This Beautiful Being is alive and has a mind of its own!" That was the first intimate greeting from my wise and Beautiful Inner Being. She was dressed in a long, flowing, glittering white gown, yet she had an androgynous face. She touched the depths of my soul with honor and love unlike anything I had ever known.

I wasn't sure what to make of that experience. Just comprehending what had happened and what it meant was all I could handle at the time. I loved my Beautiful Inner Being so! Little did I know, this was the beginning of a remarkable lifelong relationship.

I continued with my practice of meditating, primarily because I wanted the experience of my Beautiful Inner Being to return. Days went by in which I imagined her with the little me; however, the piercing look I received from her never returned. The feeling of love and connectedness stayed with me, however. My faith was strengthened; I trusted that I finally had access to a loving, wise, and compassionate entity and that she was within me at all times.

Because of this unusual experience I had in connecting with my Beautiful Inner Being, I was drawn to others who were having similar experiences. I needed my unusual experience validated. I began hearing stories about people who were visited by various forms of light. They reported that a light came in the highest form of love and had healing powers for many of them. I decided I wanted to have one of those experiences for the same reasons I wanted to fire walk. I continued to seek out experiences that would assure me that I was still connected to the God energy that had helped me with my incredible success years before.

My Angel Appears

I thought about it all the time. I imagined light pouring through me from the heavens. I tentatively invited it to visit me for the purpose of reinforcing the truth that there is an unseen force behind all things. The nature of this force is totally loving, totally protecting, totally giving, and totally present in all things at all times. I had to believe this, as that possibility allowed me to know that I could, once again, have help and assistance in my life from the highest source of all, God.

I knew I needed a divine level of assistance to pull me out of my downward spiral. My situation felt as critical to me as if I had developed something as life-threatening as cancer. I really came to believe I had been living the effects of something as serious as a debilitating or terminal disease.

One night I was suddenly awakened from a deep sleep by a streak of bright yellow light flashing across my wall between two windows, from right to left, disappearing into my bedside lamp, leaving it flashing on and off. The lamp had heat sensors and normally came on with a gentle touch. There were no hands gently touching this lamp in the middle of the night! My heart raced from the flash and surprise of the light, while at the same time I felt a power in the room, a presence that I knew protected me and loved me deeply. I felt as if the intensity could have been much stronger, but it was holding back. The force in the room seemed to know me and how much I could handle.

The next day, while trying to assimilate what had happened, I realized that I'd had my light experience! I noticed sudden changes in how I felt and reacted to certain things which had previously frightened me. For example, my daughter's boyfriend had a pet python. Visiting them later that day, for the first time I found myself able to approach the snake without feeling fear and trepidation. I actually felt kindly toward the snake, as if it were a friend. I came away from that experience feeling, once again, connected to a power far greater than I could imagine, knowing this force loved me and cared for me and was listening and responding to me.

Unfortunately, as weeks passed by, these moments of feeling connected started to disappear. My mind returned to fixating on thoughts of worry and concern about what I was really going to do with my life and how I was going to meet next month's expenses. I felt such resistance to the idea of returning to the workforce to get a JOB. This meant that I was backsliding into a void of my past that I had worked so hard to get away from.

The Power in Forgiveness and Acceptance

I had finally run out of my resources. Reaching out for help seemed like my only way out. A phone call to my daughter, Sheri, put my reality into a cold, harsh perspective. All that I had been focusing on that I didn't want to happen was happening, just as precisely as I was imagining! The Law of Attraction had not been ignoring my constant thoughts of worry and intense feelings of dread and anger about what seemed like a leaping plunge downward and backward. My doubt had returned and my life was reflecting it!

"Hi, Sheri. This is so hard for me to ask, but I need a big favor from you. Would you lend me $500 for a couple of weeks? I have decided to move back to Santa Fe yet again." I sighed, feeling so ashamed and embarrassed. It was as if I were a human yo-yo, bouncing back and forth between two cities sixty miles apart. "My dear friend Mark has graciously offered me a position in his title company, and I have decided to take him up on it. I've gone through all my money and I really appreciate your helping me out until I get paid from my new job."

This was the final straw, borrowing money from my oldest daughter. One part of me was extremely thankful she could help me out. The other part felt humiliated. How could I be in such a mess? I was constantly plagued with my critical thoughts and feelings of disgust. I felt so angry with the direction my life had taken and with my inability to turn it around. Doing what I loved seemed so far out of reach.

I was on my way back to Santa Fe again, this time to stay with my dearest friends, Jann and John. Jann was always there, reaching out in the most nonjudgmental, understanding way. I needed all the emotional support I could get, as I wasn't giving much to myself. Jann's care and acceptance soothed my tender, bruised ego.

It wasn't long after I returned to Santa Fe and began to work for my friend Mark that I began to feel a sense of relief from my financial strain. I still had no idea how to resolve the ever-growing IRS debt, though. I couldn't think about it without panicking, so I didn't. The anger, although suppressed most of the time, continued to eat at me, taking me down into the depths of depression again. Of course, I missed my daughters immensely. I lived for the weekends when I could be with them in Albuquerque. They sensed my pain and feared what they saw happening to my life. I felt so ashamed being this kind of example for them.

The nights were so long, the days so empty. I scared myself with hopeless thoughts that I couldn't endure this part of my life any longer. I had been out of touch with my Beautiful Inner Being in all my anger. One lonely, depressed night, as I contemplated swallowing a little bottle of pills and ending my life, as that seemed like the only ticket to peace, I sensed Sheri's and Lori's spirits very close to me. The warm sweep of love that embraced my shoulders reminded me that I would never hurt my daughters. I knew I wouldn't, and I felt strength just in knowing how much I loved them and how much they needed me. I chose to live. I knew I really wanted to live, and somehow I would turn everything around. I just had to for my precious daughters.

Five months passed, and I decided I was emotionally and financially stable enough to be on my own. I moved into an apartment near the freeway to Albuquerque, so I could feel a little closer to my daughters. Emotionally, this helped me stay strong. My apartment was sparsely furnished with the help of my friends. Day to day is how I lived. I still couldn't seem to shake the anger I felt boiling deep inside me.

My evenings were spent, once again, reading everything I could find on the subject of "creating"—how to use the powers of our mind to create the life we want. I was obsessed with my search for answers.

One night, while sitting up in bed, my journal on one side and a book on prosperity by Catherine Ponder on the other, I came to a place in her book where she talked about the Law of Attraction. This must have been the third time I had read this particular book, but that night her message to let go of the past and forgive came through very strong. I understood only too well how this powerful law in our universe works. That was the very principle I had worked with to miraculously sell my homes in 30 days!

There was one major difference; I felt a lot of love during those times. I hadn't been feeling much love for a very long time because I just couldn't let go of my anger. I decided to consider the possibility that my anger was messing up my life and perhaps the circumstances were only following what had been the focus of my attention for the past three and a half years!

I looked out into the room of my small apartment and in utter surprise shook my head in disbelief. I asked myself, "How could I have created everything I don't want in my life, and it's exactly what I am experiencing now?" I didn't want to be in Santa Fe and I was; I didn't want to be alone and I was; I didn't want to barely survive and I was; I didn't want to be fifteen pounds overweight and I was; I didn't want the black car I was driving; and I didn't want to feel depressed most of the time and I was. On and on my list went.

I decided to consider whether or not I had totally let go of my old expectations about my parents—expectations of how they should have provided me with a normal, emotionally healthy childhood. I gave myself permission to feel my truth. I had a lot of "should" language going on in my head. I felt guilty for not feeling forgiveness for my parents about my childhood. I found it difficult to admit and feel my negative, angry feelings and my heart full of blame.

Old memories flooded my mind and transported me back in time to one of the most profound moments that shaped the experiences I was having.

There I sat, a little 13-year-old girl, wishing I could be invisible, scared to death about revealing the truth of what was happening to me, and feeling very vulnerable and anxious that I would be judged as a terrible little girl. I remember staring into the front of a huge, hand-carved wooden desk, barely able to breathe or to take in what was happening. I felt overwhelmed by this monstrous desk that seemed to be looming over me. Worse yet, behind it sat a very large, overpowering man, Dr. M. While he seemed like an intimidating giant to me, I did have a wee bit of hope that he could help me out of my desperate situation of being molested.

I felt so small and intimidated, so wrong and embarrassed, as I recounted the shameful abuse I was experiencing to this psychiatrist, who intimidated me beyond words. Little did I know that this disturbing office visit would become one of the most defining moments that would dramatically shape a huge part of my life!

My memories are not clear as to exactly what Dr. M. said to me so many decades ago. However, I can clearly recall this man's parting words to me in front of my mother, "I am going to help you 'cope' with your situation."

"What? You're going to help me 'cope'??" I thought to myself! I was shocked. I couldn't fully absorb what this doctor was saying to me. I just knew, with every fiber of my being, that I was not going to learn to "cope" with being molested!

I concluded that Dr. M.'s plan to help me learn to cope was a way to keep me from being so upset and emotionally damaged. While I'll never know exactly what he intended, the damage was done.

My fate was sealed deep in my psyche. My feelings of being forsaken by Dr. M. and my parents were deepened by my conclusion that I was alone, with no one to protect me, no one to save me, and no one to love me. Unfortunately, my conclusions set me up to have a life of relationship disasters, betrayals, and disappointments, all of which brought me even more shame!

What I needed was protection. What I got was an offer to learn how to "cope" with a devastating situation in which I had no power or control. I made a vow that I would see to it that someday I would create my own loving environment and that I would have my own special family. I would love and protect my children no matter what. I would make a better home life for myself and for the children I hoped I would have.

I closed my heart, buried my shame, and allowed my anger to provide me with the fuel that I needed to strengthen my rebellion. The only way that I knew to protect myself was to keep my heart closed, my shame numbed, and to let my anger fight for me. This way I could maintain the illusion that I had no shame, that I was a "normal" person, and that I would someday escape this horror that I was experiencing.

Unfortunately, my anger didn't know when to stop. As I grew older, my intimate relationships reflected my perspective, which was that of a powerless victim. This perpetuated my cycle of anguish and pain for years. My subconscious conditioning was set and running, as I went through one failed marriage after another.

As my beliefs and conditioning would have it, the men who showed up in my life, those to whom I was attracted, cheated on me, used me for my money, failed to honor their financial responsibilities, or abandoned me and my two precious daughters. As if I hadn't been shamed and threatened enough, one of my husbands actually threatened me with a gun and held me and my two daughters hostage for six hours because I was leaving him.

Unfortunately, this ugly list goes on. These devastating experiences continued to add fuel to my fiery anger, an anger that I tried so hard to suppress. My ongoing negative experiences with men provided me all the evidence I needed to prove that my deep-seated beliefs about myself were true: that I was defective, unlovable, wrong, less than others, not normal, not worthy, not important, and not wanted. I was a loser.

And, when it came to men, well, I was certain that men would only look out for themselves; they would never really love me or care about me. They could only think of themselves. Men would see to it that they always got what they wanted with no regard for me (or other women) at all. I felt completely alone and feared that I would never have a normal, happy life.

As I write this, I am struck by the brilliance and love of Spirit to have blessed me with the relentless desire to have a loving, committed relationship in which I am happy, healthy, and adored. This was a constant and compelling desire that rooted itself into my heart. It would not let me rest until it was fulfilled.

This heartfelt desire eventually saved me from remaining trapped in my victim perspective, which imprisoned my soul, stunted my growth, and rendered me powerless and out of control of my life. It was not until I embodied the truth about myself and the power of love that I was able to manifest my desire to have a love in my life. This is why I knew I had to forgive my parents!

As I continued with my meditation that night in my apartment when I was hit with a profound dose of reality, I knew that forgiveness was the only way out of remaining imprisoned by my childhood subconscious conditioning. Yet something inside me would not let me forgive. As I repeated this affirmation aloud, "I stop blaming my father for hurting me in the past, and I unconditionally love him," I suddenly felt a twinge in the pit of my stomach that sent electric surges through my chest, as if a heavy force were collapsing in on me. With my eyes closed and my attention focused on the feeling, I asked, "Who inside is not willing to forgive my dad? Please come forward and talk to me. I feel you are the angry one, and I want to hear what you have to say." I got a picture in my mind of a little face peeking out of a dark corner, feeling surprised that I would be interested in listening to what she had to say. I imagined myself looking at her lovingly as I repeated my original question. "Why do you refuse to let go of your angry energy? What would it mean if you let go of me?" I stayed with the image and with my awareness of the angry feelings, while at the same time noticing the compassion I felt for this little angry one.

Dropping deeper and deeper into my trance, I felt a response from my anger saying to me, "I saved you from an abusive environment when you were young. I am the one who fired you up to finally leave your home in the midst of your enormous fear and confusion. You were too frozen without me. I am keeping you from feeling your shame and from being powerless."

With profound understanding, I said, "You are still trying to save me and keep me safe just like before, and the only way you know how is to use the energy of anger!" I sensed a very tired, yet determined, "Yes." For the first time in my life, I felt so much love coming to me from a feeling I had so denied and judged to be wrong. I sensed this pattern of reaction was repeating its intention of keeping me safe by keeping me angry. I then found myself saying, "Thank you for doing your best to protect me in the only way you knew how at the time. I know you are a pattern and you, by nature, can only repeat what you were formed to do when I was a little girl. This is why you think you have to keep me angry at my father, and all other men, for that matter." I felt another relieved

"Yes" from this angry one. I somehow knew that understanding this reactive pattern, not fighting with it or making it wrong, was the perfect way to be. I felt a great relief. Being empathetic with this little angry one felt loving and right.

A thought then occurred to me: I should send my anger new information. "I want to introduce you to a new type of energy that is now going to take care of me for the rest of my life." I imagined a huge beam of bluish, shimmering light appearing as an angel, pouring into my mind from the right side, as both the little angry one and I looked on.

"You are tired and I am letting your words dissolve, as your anger is bringing me everything I don't want, and I know you want me to feel happy, safe, and protected. I want you to meet the God energy of love and wisdom. This is the energy that created me. I'm in the best of hands, so I no longer need to be protected with your angry thoughts of how things should have been. I am now protected with love."

I then imagined this little ball of anger melting into the rays of the loving, brilliant light. As I brought my attention back to the room, I was awestruck at what had just happened. "Where did all of that come from?" I thought. I felt so much love and harmony. I sensed the presence of my Beautiful Inner Being prompting me through the entire exercise and my loving and powerful angel bathing me in unconditional love.

What a gift this was, for I had never had the courage or know-how to face my anger and lovingly understand its function—how it was just trying to keep me intact by responding with anger, as it had done so many years ago!

The next morning as I left my apartment for work, I knew I would be in charge of my life in a way I had never known before, and somehow I would have what I wanted. I knew I had made that new decision with absolute conviction in my heart.

In the days following, I became consumed with designing my life exactly as I wanted it to be. I made a list of everything I had been wanting. I started by writing down all the attributes I wanted in a committed relationship with the man of my dreams, as detailed as the color of his hair, the activities we would share, and the lifestyle we would enjoy. Next, I wrote about the new place where I wanted to live in Albuquerque. I knew exactly where it was. I had discovered it during a visit with my daughters. I had no idea, however, how I would afford it. I only knew then that I was going to have it. I didn't hold back with what I wanted.

Next, I wrote about a new car. I wanted a new red convertible (obviously a memory of my red Mercedes I'd reluctantly sold). I listed the amount I wanted to spend each month. I had no idea how I would pull this off with my bankruptcy looming over me from just two years earlier. Again, I didn't care that I didn't know, at least in that moment.

I decided this was enough to start with, but in no way was this the last word on my life. I still had the IRS debt looming over my head and an unsolved mystery as to which direction my career as a designer/creator would lead. I knew there would be much to learn in creating and attracting my chosen desires. These definitely felt like priorities, as I felt the strongest urge to have them. I chose dates when I wanted to realize each of my desires. I decided on one month for my relationship, two months for the new apartment in Albuquerque, and three months for the car. My work was cut out for me, and so I began.

I followed the practice of daily visualizing the final outcomes of my desires. As a matter of fact, it became more of an obsession than a daily practice. I remembered the process I followed when I was selling my homes. I knew that feeling love for what I was creating was the most appropriate, most effective way to bring these things into my life.

I thought I trusted enough in the Law of Attraction and that it would, once again, work for me to help me realize what I wanted. I now realized something very important. I must always find the ingredient of feeling love and appreciation while imagining what I want to create. I reflected on my experiences of "magically" selling my premium homes. I knew I had to capture what I had learned about using the power of the subconscious mind to create what I wanted. This time, I just couldn't leave anything out.

Negative talk reeked among many Santa Fe real estate agents, with comments like, "Things are really slow right now. They aren't even putting up signs in some areas because it looks like a fire sale." I knew what I was up against, but I felt so sure about my work, and based on my metaphysical studies, I just knew my home would sell quickly. I had purchased another property in Albuquerque, which was set to close in sixty days, so I had a strong reason to focus on a quick sale for the price I wanted.

The Power in Forgiveness and Acceptance

I listed my premium custom home with a friend, Fran, and we set our sights for a November 1986 closing. Fortunately, she also believed that we could easily attract the perfect buyer, so I had an ally to rely on to support me in my outrageous proclamation, "My home will be sold in thirty days!" This took a lot of nerve for me to say, particularly because most of my friends were in the real estate business, and being embarrassed by overconfidence and looking foolish was the last thing I wanted to feel. There was, however, a quiet confidence deep within my soul that I knew what I was doing. I knew how to visualize what I wanted; I knew I loved my home, and I was willing to let it go. I was excited to move on. I just knew, somehow, that everything would come together.

Days went by, and I held to my vision of the sale taking place. I imagined the people walking through my home, completely moved by its spirited energy. I felt complete awe and appreciation for the beauty and specialness that permeated my home from the moment I stepped on the grounds. I would walk across the shining Saltillo floors in amazement and marvel that I had created this magnificent home. As a little girl, back home in Columbia, Missouri, I always dreamed, while walking through the subdivision my father built, that someday I would have a home as beautiful as the homes he built for others. And, behold, there I was standing in my dream.

As time passed and I seriously began approaching my thirty-day mark, I began feeling anxiety, with sharp pains moving up from my throat and into my face. Doubt and concern were moving in, especially when stating my proclamation, "My home will be sold in thirty days," to my family and friends. As I held on to my statement,

I silently heard my rational mind telling me how crazy I was to believe such a thing, because, after all, the odds were completely against the likelihood of this happening.

No one in their right mind would have ever counted on a thirty-day sale, especially in this price range! Had I lost my mind? I had a lot at stake by now, not only with the embarrassment should this sale not happen, but worse yet, the contract I had signed for my next land purchase didn't allow for any contingencies. That felt very threatening to me. It was getting more and more difficult for me to concentrate on the process. Finally, one bright, sunny afternoon, one day past my thirty-day goal, I angrily stormed out of the house, fearful because my home had not yet sold. I threw myself into my red Mercedes convertible, muttering under my breath, "I've got to get out of here. This is all too much. I just give up. I've done everything I can possibly do."

I believed in the Law of Attraction, and I had cooperated as best as I knew how. I felt hopeless and tired. My rational mind had taken over. I began wondering if I was crazy to believe that something so simple and magical could really be true. I drove and drove, trying to understand why my home had not sold. I believed in the power of God's energy. I had put so much on the line. "I just give up. It truly is up to God now." I sighed.

After about an hour, I returned home, only to discover a visitor had arrived while I was busy with my tantrum. A woman looking at homes in our neighborhood strolled down our road, and when she saw our home was for sale, decided to come in. As she entered the foyer, looking up with a smile, she remarked, "This is exactly what I have been looking for all day. I didn't think I would ever find a home like this in Santa Fe." She sighed with a look of relief. We had a contract the next day and closed in time for me to meet my new purchase deadline.

My confidence grew in this process, and once again, a year and a half later, I found myself making that same grand proclamation for the next home I decided to sell in Albuquerque, just sixty miles south of Santa Fe. I had also designed this home, so my feeling of love for it, almost like the love felt for a child, was very easy to hold. I knew that once I experienced this process of attracting the perfect buyers to my homes consistently, I would never doubt again.

I faced the doubt of the real estate community again, just as I always did in Santa Fe. As in my past experiences, premium estate homes were not selling in my area until they had been on the market a year or so. I dared to be bold and say, "My home will be sold in thirty days." I felt confident this time because of my previous successes. Of course, my listing agent just went along with me to humor my seemingly crazy and outrageous thinking.

I continued my visualizations daily; I felt the love for my beautiful home and trusted in this process I had come to know. Again, the days went by quietly, with very few people looking at my home. I kept my faith until the thirtieth day approached and passed. This time I had a construction loan due, and the consequences of not paying it off were too awful for me to consider. My faith in my connection with what I knew to be a very special power was diminishing rapidly. What had I done wrong this time?

Deep confusion set in, and one night, after thirty-five days, I burst into tears and sobs that lasted for two hours. I had been ignoring and resisting my feelings of hopelessness and fear and feeling as though I had been abandoned. It was not only that my home had not sold. More importantly, I had lost faith in the greatest source of my life—that source being God's energy that brings life to all things, including the desires of my heart. I was losing faith in my belief system which gave me a sense of security. Again, the feeling that I had to give up and truly let go of the strain of this entire process was all I had left within me.

The next couple of days, I felt a little more relaxed. I knew I had done all I could and I would have to believe everything was happening for the best, although I had no earthly idea what that might be at the time. I just continued to love my home. I truly appreciated the opportunity to create such a magnificent place, and I knew it would be wonderful for someone, someday. Meanwhile, I was certainly enjoying it myself.

Thirty-seven days passed, and one afternoon, while I was finishing some painting in the entryway, a delightful-looking couple approached our front door and asked if they could please come in and look around. They were apologetic for not having an appointment. Normally I would have been so excited that someone showed up. However, this time I calmly invited them in and told them they were free to look around. I suddenly felt a warm glow in my heart and just knew these people were going to buy my house. Sure enough, I had a contract the next day! We closed on May 22, which allowed the loan to be paid off on May 25. Wow, this time I knew I would never doubt again.

The Power in Forgiveness and Acceptance

It seemed I needed to see results over and over again from this process that I had stumbled onto about focusing my mind to create what I wanted before I could really come to accept it.

I knew, after my visit with the "angry one," how detrimental it was to resist my anger and fears by repressing and denying them, just as I had done with my experiences of selling my homes, and denying my resentment and anger with my parents for so many years. Resisting my negative emotions had significantly affected my life in disastrous ways. I learned my lessons well; it does not serve my life to expect others to change or behave in certain ways. That only leads to fueling my anger more while leaving me with profound disappointment and heartache, not to mention a crazy, upside-down life.

I came to realize that other people can only do what they have the emotional capacity to do, just as my unconscious pattern of anger could only do what it was designed to do—to generate angry energy that moved me into action. Unfortunately, this survival pattern created more anger in me that I had to suppress, which subsequently brought me more disasters throughout my early life.

I gained an understanding of the unmet needs I had as a child. I found a better way to fulfill those needs with love, not fear. I was blessed with a sense of compassion and understanding as to how my anger was just a way for me to reach out for love. I realized my parents were subconsciously reaching out for love, too. Through my inner work and my growing faith in the power of love from Spirit, I was able to accept that it was their unconscious programming that drove them to the behaviors and choices that they made.

A few weeks went by and, behold, a new man showed up in my life. I learned a lot from that brief relationship. You cannot fool Mother Nature, the natural creative power of the subconscious mind. I was still unaware of the subconscious lack of acceptance I had for my body and of the fear I had about being in another relationship. I constantly focused on "being too fat." I felt anxious because I believed I was not going to attract the man of my dreams while being fifteen pounds overweight. I know that sounds a little crazy, yet that's how powerful these beliefs are.

My obsessive worry that I was too heavy to be accepted and loved is what created this man, interestingly enough, who was obsessed with wanting a woman who was thin! He didn't like heavy women any more than I liked myself.

I could not bring myself to be fully present with him. My constant, critical worry that I wasn't good enough haunted me, leading me to believe that he would eventually leave me for a thinner woman. I imagined that, quietly in his mind, he was criticizing me. This kept me self-conscious and defensive most of the time. My crazy thinking was reinforced by his concern in wanting to help me lose weight.

Another little hidden secret Mother Nature knew was how inferior I still felt about not making the large income I had earned in the past. I pretended to be okay on the surface, while my feelings of unworthiness, which I had denied, seethed deep within me. I dared not admit this to myself, for that would have validated my feelings of inferiority, and the shame of that was only to be kept buried deep within me.

This man talked about business success and money constantly. I longed for feelings of acceptance, closeness, security and well-being. What I felt in this relationship was quite the opposite. I decided that attracting the man of my dreams who adored and loved me was going to be more difficult than I had thought. I was filled with confusion and disappointment, for what I thought I knew about attracting still wasn't enough. It seemed easier to let go of this desire for now and focus on my move, once again, back to Albuquerque, back to my daughters.

The "Magic" Reappears

I was lifted and encouraged by thoughts of being closer to my daughters once again. I felt a warmth and sense of well-being just thinking about being near them and living in the luxury apartment complex that I really loved. I had visited this apartment complex each time I was in Albuquerque. I felt myself living there very easily. I had a strong conviction that I would surely be living there very soon, regardless of the long waiting list.

On one weekend visit, I was inspired to inquire as to the availability of a particular apartment that I liked within this complex. I had my list of everything I wanted. Everything matched except the price, of course! I was so definite that I wanted to be there. I kept my focus and belief on the thought, "I will be living here soon, somehow." I completed an application and allowed myself to be put on their waiting list. I was told it might be a few months.

One week later, I received a phone call from the woman with whom I had left my application. She announced, "I have just received notice that a woman is getting married and she'll be vacating her apartment in thirty days. It matches the description you gave me of what you want."

She told me that she was eager to call me right away, and informed me that if I would put a deposit on the apartment, I could have it. "The first person to place a deposit gets the apartment," she explained. My heart raced with joy, but I immediately fell into a panic. "This is so soon," I thought. "How will I get to Albuquerque fast enough to secure the apartment, and how will I ever afford it?" Now was the time to think about that minor little detail. I decided to elicit the help of my daughters.

I called and asked Sheri and Lori if they would go to the apartment complex immediately and give this woman a deposit of $100 to secure the apartment. I assured them I would reimburse them. I expressed my complete trust in them to preview the apartment for me. I had only seen a copy of the floor plan. Lori suddenly popped up with a surprising request. "Mom, I've been thinking. I would like to know if you would consider letting me live with you again. My roommate has recently told me she is leaving, and I don't know what I'm going to do! You and I are both alike in our tastes. So, what do you say? We could help each other by sharing the expenses."

Tears welled up in my eyes as I felt a warm sense of relief come over me. "Yes, of course you can," I answered, sensing the work of a miracle. Lori's contribution as my roommate eased the financial strain. I now had a profound experience of the synchronization that occurs in creating. I felt comforted in knowing I had the assistance of the power I had come to trust years ago! "Could it be I'm getting back on track again?" I thought.

I had a deep sense that I was finally on to this creating business, more skilled and aware than I had ever been before. "What's working?" I pondered. "What's the difference that has allowed me to attract this apartment so easily and quickly, unlike my relationship that brought me so much pain and anguish?" I was determined to continue my quest for the answers, which seemed to elude me at the time. Content in the moment, I enjoyed the glow from the miracle I had just been given.

The girls secured the apartment for me that day. Later that night, Lori phoned and informed me that the location of the apartment was exactly what I wanted; it faced east toward the mountains! She was as excited to move in with me as I was to have her. It was truly magical!

I now had a strong reason to focus on the car I had previously written about on my list of things I wanted. I was going to be commuting from Albuquerque to my work in Santa Fe, and I didn't feel safe in my car. I was chipping away at all of the things I no longer wanted in my life. My confidence and self-esteem were rising to healthier levels than ever before. I felt a sense of control, yet I was still very cautious about the changes that were happening.

I began looking at every car on the road, just to see what I liked and didn't like. Could I actually find what I was seeing in my mind or something even better? I was willing to go for it. I had come too far to give up now. I did notice, however, a very subtle, nagging feeling of worry that I might have a problem getting a loan. It had only been two years since my bankruptcy was granted, and the IRS debt was still ever-present in my life. I knew there had to be a way.

While driving down the road one day, I caught a glimpse of a little red convertible sitting on a car lot. I made a sudden turn into the dealership, realizing that I was entering a place in which I had a friend who happened to be the manager! I knew Dennis from one of the mountain retreats I had been on four years earlier. We had climbed up poles and jumped off cliffs together. We had remained friends over the past four years. "What a relief," I thought. My situation was embarrassing enough. "Dennis will understand and help me as best he can," I said to myself, feeling a strong sense of trust that rekindled my hope.

One of his salespeople worked out a deal that required me to pay $4,000 down, with monthly payments in the amount I wanted. The large down payment was needed to counter my previous bankruptcy and to allow me to build up my credit once again. "Perfect", I thought. The perfect car, perfect payments, but not-so-perfect down payment. Now what was I going to do? I was beside myself, although still very determined I would create the money somehow.

I wrote out a check for $4,000 and dated it thirty days later.

Dennis said he would hold it for me until then. I drove off the lot, temporarily excited about my new red convertible. I tried not to let the thought that I was out of my mind to think I could really pull this off linger in my head. I stayed focused on exactly what must appear by August 18, my deadline, feeling determined it was going to work out. There was something magical about these thirty-day creations for me!

Despite the doubts and concerns of my friends that I even dared reveal this to, I stayed focused. "It has to work. I've come too far, and I believe in this process of attracting what I choose into my life. If I believe this is so, then I must act like it's so," I thought with a renewed sense of conviction. I was really testing my faith at a level I hadn't experienced since my home sales, four years earlier.

A few weeks later, while having dinner with my mother, I had a strong impulse to ask her if she would be willing to lend me the money for the down payment on my new car. I was fairly okay in asking, as I felt confident I could pay her back. I suspected this would not create a financial problem for her, as she was financially sound. It was a real stretch for me to reach out for help and not think I was a failure. I knew I was putting my life back in order and I had spent a fortune trying just about everything to help me do just that. My mother recognized my diligent attempts to release the painful beliefs that I had generated long ago and how committed I was to healing. She said she would think it over and call me later that night.

I left the restaurant feeling as though I was going to faint with relief. I felt so appreciative of her acknowledging my intense efforts to let go of the painful, erroneous beliefs from my past. That meant more to me than the money. I felt loved and accepted in a way I had never experienced from her before.

Later that night, she called. "Judy, I've been thinking. I will give you the money only if you take it as a gift. I will not lend it to you. You deserve a break after all you have been through." Tears welled up in my eyes. My throat stung. I was unable to talk. I mumbled with disbelief, "Thank you so much, Mom. I really intended to borrow the money, not take it from you. Are you sure it's all right?"

She responded emphatically, "I wouldn't have offered if it wasn't okay."

This was the evening of August 17. My check was to be deposited the next day. This timing was a strong statement to me of the synchronization that occurs within the creative process. It never occurred to me in the beginning that my mom would have been the one to give me the money, especially in such a generous way.

So many times I thought I would never doubt again. This was truly a miracle. The love and support I felt from my mom was truly the gift this miracle brought. I knew I had achieved that same level of love and support for myself or this would not have happened. "Thank you, God," I repeated over and over, feeling so appreciative, not just about my life coming together, but about the magnificent "creative process" I was discovering and the love for myself and others it brought.

With the healing and creative process I was learning, often the hard way, I knew I would resolve what seemed to be my problem in attracting a romantic relationship. I now had a way to create a clear path toward the relationship of my dreams. This would require more love for myself and less fear of being in a committed relationship. For that moment, however, I was totally content, feeling a sense of well-being deep within my soul. I was connected to the source of all things and I was now beginning to see how truly giving the nature of God really is!

Summer was ending, and fall was quickly approaching. My move back to Albuquerque opened a new awareness that more of my life would be changing. I knew the commute of 120 miles back and forth to Santa Fe each day would get very old, particularly in the winter months. I felt a sense of completion of my year in Santa Fe—an end of the anger and guilt that were triggered by many of my experiences during that year. I had peacefully let go of the mistaken beliefs that generated my angry, guilty, and shameful feelings about the negative experiences in my childhood.

I had a feeling all along that my purpose in coming back to Santa Fe was to face and dissolve these negative patterns that I had ignored for so long. These patterns of judgment reflected my need to be right. Holding on to my expectations of how parents should act gave me a false sense that I should be loved and accepted and that I was somehow entitled to have a normal life. I had idealized thoughts of what a normal life should be like.

My experience of compassionately talking with my anger and discovering its method of protecting me, dissolving it into the light, and choosing a new means to satisfy my unmet needs with love, not anger and fear, changed all of that. I had come closer than ever before to what I imagined unconditional love could be.

I truly knew in my heart that my parents did the best they could at the time. I felt so much love and compassion for all of us. I had come to understand how unconscious I was of certain decisions I had made as a child in reacting to frightening and confusing experiences. I made these decisions about myself and my life in the hope that they would lead to me feeling safe and secure.

It was not until I experienced my healing process that I understood why I subconsciously continued to generate thoughts that kept me feeling angry and guilty. These subconscious patterns were designed to protect me by making my parents wrong. My unmet expectations generated deep feelings of anger that provided me with a temporary sense of power. My guilty thoughts and feelings were designed to avoid my feelings of hurt and shame.

I received new information in my miraculous meditation process: my power in this world comes from love, not fear. Only then was I able to make a new decision to let go of my need to judge and condemn my parents and to let the power of love and understanding penetrate every part of my being.

I knew my parents were suffering and acting out of their protective, unconscious patterns that were created from their past, fearful and unloving experiences. I was getting it. It is truly my own negative thoughts about my past that continue to cause my pain and suffering, not my past experiences! No one is sentenced to be victimized by their past.

It was through facing and accepting my feelings that I accessed my inner truths. I then had the ability to bring about permanent changes in my life. This process turned my life around faster than anything I had ever known. I knew I had begun to do just that. This is why I have come to believe that the healing process is an essential part of the "art of manifesting."

Results were showing up one right after the other, and I was feeling better about myself than ever before. I was no longer a powerless victim but one who was at the helm of my life as its co-creator. My decision to let go of the need to be right and to understand the hurts and fears of my parents allowed me to love them unconditionally. This brought me a profound sense of peace and well-being.

My Journey into the Depths of Contrast

The next challenge that moved to the front burner of my life was changing my work environment from Santa Fe to Albuquerque. This was a fearful thought, for I had no extra money saved to sustain me from the time I left my job in Santa Fe until I found a suitable position in Albuquerque. Soon after making the decision to change my work, I received a call from a friend, Judy, who had also decided to make a job change.

We were both intense about doing what we love for a living. We just weren't quite sure of what form it would take. We decided to do the next best thing and go somewhere we loved, Hawaii. Now, I know I intended to work in Albuquerque. After all, my beautiful apartment and my daughters were there. I decided, however, that I needed some extra money before I moved to Albuquerque permanently. This was a new idea for me to consider—having stability in my life for a change. Judy had an idea that sounded great at the time; however, it turned into a shining example of how to create deep, dark contrast in my life. I failed to pay attention to how I was feeling during the time that I was envisioning myself being in Hawaii. I had failed to do my healing work back then.

Judy was aware of an opportunity in which we could work on a cruise ship that sailed around the Hawaiian Islands. Her daughter had the experience during the summer and had a glorious time, fell in love, and came home with a bundle of cash. This all sounded inspiring. I had once imagined living in Hawaii, and I remember saying out loud, "I would give anything to live there. I would even wait tables if I had to." Well, I was about to do just that.

Judy discovered ways in which we could easily become employed by the ship line, work in beautiful Hawaii for three months, come home for a month, and be paid! We were allured by the idea of being in Hawaii and meeting interesting people. Perhaps the man of my dreams would be found in romantic Hawaii! We hoped we would receive a lot of money in tips, and due to minimal living expenses while on the ship, we anticipated bringing home a large portion of that money. In addition, we were to be paid for the month off following our three-month shift at sea. That was my plan for being financially secure, at least for a month, while I looked for work in Albuquerque. It makes me cringe to think about this experience as I write about it.

Ironically, just before my abrupt move to Santa Fe, one year prior to this time, I had envisioned myself being in Hawaii, feeling totally carefree and happy. I was longing for peace and serenity away from the horror I was experiencing at the time. I listened to music with ocean waters crashing onto the beach, and I imagined the freedom of the seagulls flying over the ocean. I visualized the magnificent tropical flowers with their sweet fragrances permeating my nose, affecting me as an elixir, healing me from the depths of despair I was feeling at that time. I associated Hawaii with getting away from my troubles, feeling safe and secure, wrapped in the beautiful environment like a child in her mother's arms. I was still looking outside myself for feelings of safety and security, so this desire served a very strong need that I had during that time.

It was now time for the seed I had planted of being in Hawaii to be born. Apparently my need to feel safe and secure was looming over me once again, as I seriously considered leaving my current job to move on. Although I was not experiencing the panic I had felt a year earlier, the feelings of peace and security I associated with being in Hawaii were still not satisfied. My relentless need to satisfy these feelings is what influenced me to agree to participate in the adventure upon which we were about to embark.

I said good-bye to my friends in Santa Fe and I proceeded with the initial arrangements necessary to get on the ship. We were assured by an influential friend of Judy's that there would be no problem with our being hired as deck lounge stewardesses, so I felt comfortable taking the risk of leaving my job and making the journey to Hawaii. I could not conceive what it would be like to be away, so far away, from my daughters, family, and friends for three months. I had never experienced being away from them for that long. Lori did, however, begin to feel my leaving and started to panic about living alone for a while. There was nothing I could say to help her feel better, and, with our departure date quickly approaching, I had much on my mind.

Despite my daughters' attempts to change my mind, I proceeded with my plan, swept up by the images and feelings I associated with Hawaii, out of touch with the reality of what this adventure would really be like. The day finally came, and off we flew to a fabulous paradise we had constructed in our minds, safe from the worries of our world—well, so we thought.

During the first two weeks in Honolulu, we kept busy with the necessary physicals, drug tests, and interviews required for us to be hired. Our vacation in paradise began with the excitement that one would expect from any new beginning; however, by the second week my loneliness for Sheri and Lori and for my life back home started tugging at my heartstrings. I was starting to realize how long the next three months would be, and we hadn't yet boarded the ship! I only had the experience of the glamorous life on a cruise ship through my personal experience as a passenger. My perception of reality was about to change.

I forced myself to keep looking ahead and remember why I was there. Fortunately, Judy and I alternated our highs and lows, so we were supportive of each other. The day to board the ship finally came. I lived with fear and anxiety about the whole experience. The truth was, contrary to what I told the man that hired us, I had never been a waitress and served food or drinks in my entire life. I had to fake this one for sure! Payback time was coming. . .

We arrived at port on midday Saturday, scheduled to sail away that night with 800 passengers and return the following Saturday. We were to sail through the Hawaiian Islands at night and dock on a different island each day. My heart raced from fear anticipating the whole experience, because the reality of my new job on board that ship started getting clearer and clearer. I put my desperate thoughts aside, for I could barely hear and digest the rules we were learning. "What have we gotten ourselves into," we gasped with mounting terror and much regret.

It was time to board the ship. I looked toward the passenger ramp, anticipating that is where we would board; however, I was directed to an opening far below the passenger entrance. As we approached the opening, smells from the mounds of garbage bagged for disposal reeked so strongly that they made my eyes water. I took a deep breath, as if I knew to brace myself for something traumatic, and we slowly walked forward. My body was on guard, moving as if I were maneuvering through enemy jungles, terrified with every step I took.

We passed down a hallway when suddenly I choked and gagged. The odor was so pungent I could hardly stand it. I became sick to my stomach and fought to hold back the impulse to vomit. "What is that obnoxious smell?" I asked. Judy advised me we had just passed the diesel room below. It was hot and muggy, which made the situation worse. By now I knew I had made a grave mistake and all I could think about was getting out of there.

Praying we would share the same room, we were shown to our quarters. As our luck would have it, we were assigned different rooms. I opened the door to my room and I freaked. "I'm in a jail cell!" I gasped. No windows, two cot-like beds, one sink that was illuminated by a very dim light, and two metal cabinets which were apparently meant to house my clothing. Dark green paint, chipped with age, colored the walls and made the room seem even more drab. My heart would not stop racing with panic as I tried to stay calm. We were to report for duty in less than two hours!

We finally managed to be put in the same room. Next we had to find our way to the bottom of the ship and pick up our uniforms. We found our way into the ghastly pit of the ship. The heat must have been 110°, and the temperament of the uniform crew was equally hot.

I looked up into what seemed to be thousands of blouses, skirts, pants, shirts and shorts, varying in size from small to large. We fought our way through the jungle of clothes in a helter-skelter fashion, for time was ticking away quickly. We left this hell hole in a state of frenzy as we returned to our quarters in preparation for our first assignment on deck.

We had been briefed on which uniform was appropriate for the evening shift. As I held the long black skirt up to my waist, it continued to flow about 8 inches beyond my feet. "Oh no!" I muttered beneath my breath. I could hardly think straight, for I was in such a state of panic. I remembered I had brought a needle and thread. "Thank God!" I thought. I didn't have time to fully appreciate the last-minute decision to bring that little sewing kit, but I don't know what I would have done without it.

It took me five minutes just to thread the needle. I was shaking so hard I couldn't hold it. I finally pulled myself together enough to steady my hands. My insides were vibrating so fast, I felt as if I would explode right out of my skin.

Somehow I hemmed the skirt and pulled myself together just in time to find the very small, very old elevator that took us to the upper-level decks where we were to report for our shift. This was the environment I was familiar with—as a passenger. "I am on the wrong side of the ship," I thought, feeling further regret for my decision to come to Hawaii under these conditions. I related more with the passengers than the crew members, given the sub-human living quarters assigned to the crew members.

We listened intently to the bar manager as he recited the rules and routines we were expected to observe. Off we went to our assigned tables to serve drink orders well into the wee hours of the morning. I was beginning to calm down a little, for the more I interacted with the passengers, the more at ease I felt. Turning in drink orders to the bartenders was a totally different experience, however. I was about to become indoctrinated into a world I had never known—a sailor's life on board ship. The language alone was repulsive.

I approached the counter with my first drink order and awaited my turn, only to discover that the bartender had no patience with me not knowing exactly how to call the drink orders and how to garnish the Hawaiian drinks appropriately. It was clear to me that he was not going to be my teacher, either. After all, I was supposed to know this stuff. Now my faking it became most obvious. I wondered if I would ever get through this alive! The bartender might kill me in the bowels of this ship late one night. And this was happening in "paradise"?

The first night finally ended at 1:00 a.m. Judy and I crawled back to the lower levels of the ship, walked into our cabin, and were reminded that this place was not a bad dream; it was real. I hadn't eaten all day. I was still suffering from the pungent smell of diesel fuel and I couldn't swallow anything!

Our dining area was located just around the corner from the entrance to the pit, the engine room. As I fell into my bed, tears from exhaustion and regret flooded my eyes as I silently washed away into sleep.

The next day promised to be brighter, as Judy and I made plans to see Hawaii after our day shift ended. We pleaded for the same schedules, and fortunately, somehow we touched the bar manager's heart. Actually, I think we were so pathetically misplaced, even the most insensitive person would have done no less. I could barely think about getting through each day, although I did the best I could. I dared not think about how lost and out of place I was, for that would have undoubtedly consumed me.

As I became increasingly exposed to some of the crew members, particularly those who were approaching the end of their three-month stretch, I gained a deeper understanding of the phrase, "They swear like sailors." I had never heard such vile language, not even in school. Judy and I both shared the thought that we felt old enough to be most of these people's mothers. This type of work seemed to attract young kids in college who would break away for a while to earn extra money for school. There were no living expenses on the ship, so it was quite feasible to save money. After all, that was why we were there too!

Our second day of sailing was the first opportunity to explore the islands, as we were assigned an earlier shift. I could hardly wait to disembark onto still, solid ground. I spotted public telephones just off to my right. I bolted down the gangplank, thinking only of hearing my daughters' precious voices.

The line for the phones seemed to go on forever, although I was prepared to wait as long as it took. Finally, I was dialing Lori's number, praying she would be home. I was deeply concerned about how she was adjusting to being alone in the apartment, and I painfully missed her. Four rings and she answered. My throat choked up and started to burn from my attempt to hold back the gasping sobs, while I tried to speak as if I were okay.

"Mom, are you okay?" she asked with panic in her voice. "You sound like you're crying. What is happening to you over there? When are you coming home? This is just not working. Please come home," she pleaded again and again. I couldn't say a word without bursting into a deep sobbing cry. It took me forever to open my mouth and respond to her in a way that was coherent, but I knew I was scaring her, so I regained my composure as quickly as I could. "I am all right, Lori," I responded with as much conviction as I could muster up. "It's just that I miss you and Sheri so much. I had no idea this would be so difficult. Let's give this some time. I don't know what else I can do. Please tell Sheri I called and I'm okay." My voice cracked as I said, "I love you both." The tears started welling up inside. Sensing I was about to lose it again, I quickly said good-bye and hurried off to be alone and cry.

Judy was having the same difficulty as I was with this little adventure of ours. We tried to reassure each other that things would get better as we adjusted to our new life at sea. Hundreds of passengers we talked to found themselves entertained by the story in which "Judy and Judy" uprooted themselves and set out to sail throughout the Hawaiian Islands (especially at our ages). Thinking about it took us aback a little ourselves. "Maybe this was a courageous endeavor, after all, I pondered.

My fleeting courage quickly left as we set sail with the second group of 800 passengers the following week. We were exhausted from working so hard the first week, and there we were, doing it all over again! We were not entitled to any days off during our three-month stretch. After our first week of ship duty, I was ready to quit! My ankles were beginning to swell from the humidity, and standing on my feet for ten to fourteen hours a day didn't help matters either. The beautiful island paradise was being consumed by a relentless, tormenting adversity, which certainly didn't match my picture of what I was to experience in Hawaii. I was more upset in Hawaii than I would have been had I risked moving directly to Albuquerque, trusting I would find work very quickly. At least I would have been in the comforts of my own loving, familiar surroundings.

The third week of sailing with our third group of 800 passengers was about all I could stand. Judy and I were so tired that when we were off our shifts during the day, we didn't care what Hawaii looked like, much less have the energy to be on our feet. We found the most quiet, cool places where someone would wait on us for a change, and we crashed, dwelling on our thoughts of home. The ocean carried my thoughts of leaving, or, to use the proper term, jumping ship, as far as my eyes could see, somehow reaching out to touch the life I had left just six weeks before.

I knew I had learned a very important lesson about reaching outside of myself to feel better. I remembered thinking, "If only I could be in Hawaii where life is beautiful and serene, where only peace and gentleness could exist amongst such beauty. Then I would be free of my worries." Wrong!

I had longed for peace, security, and well-being, yet I felt quite the opposite. I materialized an experience in Hawaii which triggered the same feelings I was trying to escape from. Imagining an experience while feeling the opposite of what I was longing for brought me not what I wanted, but what I already had. This fit my understanding of the Law of Attraction only too well. The need for peace, contentment, and well-being was definitely high on my list, and yet it eluded me from the beginning. It was time to take care of myself and to put me where I wanted to be: home.

Judy and I honored a pact that we had made when we first arrived in Hawaii. We would stick by each other. If one wanted to stay, the other would stay. Likewise, if one wanted to leave, the other would leave. We had no need for a compromise in this situation. We were both so exhausted, we had no energy to force ourselves to stay and keep up the façade. Being on stage for 800 passengers each week was no longer tolerable. We made our plans to jump ship the day we arrived back in port in Honolulu.

Actually, we did let our supervisor know of our plans, and much to our surprise, he claimed he knew all along we wouldn't complete our stay. "You two have been the most sophisticated ladies we've had serving our passengers in a very long time," he said. "Next time, buy two tickets and enjoy Hawaii!" He chuckled. We agreed.

I sensed a very strong feeling that our decision to come home when we did was going to bring each of us closer to the dreams we truly desired. All we had to do was to trust and listen to our inner guidance.

As the plane landed in Albuquerque, I felt an appreciation for what I had, unlike any feeling I have ever known. It was as if I had fallen in love with my life again. Everything looked bright and filled with joy. In retrospect, my experience in Hawaii served me well by magnifying what was truly important to me: my home, family, and friends. I realized the importance of my spiritual path now more than ever. I had been called home from the depths of my soul.

My Feelings—
My Powerful Pals

Comfortable once again in the surroundings of my home, I felt a deep pull to enroll in a class to further my metaphysical studies. The feeling was so strong, I couldn't have stopped it if I'd wanted to. It was as if I was being pulled toward the idea with an intense burning desire. Much to my delight, I discovered a class was beginning in one week at the church I had frequently attended. They were still accepting registrations, so

I quickly signed up. This particular class was a study of Arnold Patent's book, *You Can Have It All!* It sounded perfect to me. I was certainly ready to "have it all" after having experienced so much contrast in Hawaii. I felt a renewed sense of hope that I had finally gotten back on track.

My out-of-the-way path home finally put me face to face with my fear of finding a suitable position in Albuquerque. I so deeply wanted to keep my focus on design and creating; however, not knowing how or where to express myself, I dismissed the concept of doing what I loved for the moment, giving in to the pressing need for money that my bank account clearly demanded.

There was still more I needed to discover about my passionate work of transformation and creating. I knew it would eventually assist me in realizing my very important dreams. For now, I was enjoying the feeling of security and peace that came as a result of handling my financial affairs and living in an environment that represented love and beauty as best I could create at the time.

I disciplined myself to begin my meditation practices again. I sensed a strong need to connect with my inner guidance. I knew I would need it to assist me in my quest for work. I was very aware and in touch with the same panic and fear that I had felt during my financial crisis a year or so before. Feelings of abandonment, panic, and despair loomed over me just as I had experienced earlier. This time, however, I was prepared to respond in a very different way. I knew my past experience of the angry little one, with whom I had dialogued about forgiveness just months before, would certainly be beneficial for me. An opportunity presented itself to utilize my healing process once again. My truths were about to unfold in a profound experience late one painful night....

I was awakened by the pounding of my heart and the throbbing of my temples. I felt as though I were being chased by a huge mountain lion, running fiercely after me, roaring as if to let me know I would be eaten alive at any moment. I broke out in a cold sweat, panicked by thoughts of being consumed. I was being eaten alive by memories of the past, thoughts of despair and worry of falling, once again, into the deep hole of fear and desperation. I remembered what I had learned in my class about separating my thoughts from my feelings. I remained focused on the energy sensations in my body as they moved up from my solar plexus into my throat. As I continued breathing slowly and deeply, I imagined that I was plucking my thoughts out of my feelings, just as a hair is plucked from the skin. The overwhelming sensations soon dissipated.

Once the attack diminished, I asked the "anxiety" to please come forward and talk to me. I felt the exasperation from this little one as I allowed the feelings to well up from the depths of my terrified being.

"What do you need to say?" I asked. "I am so sorry for ignoring you for so long and denying your demands for attention. What do you want me to know?" I sensed a distrust from this little one, as if I wasn't going to be believed. "What do you need from me that would calm you and let you know I am listening to you?" I asked.

From the depths of my heart, an inner voice replied, "I need you to pay attention to our security and basic matters of the world.

I'm so afraid you will not take the action necessary to take care of us, just as before, when we had to move to Santa Fe and we bottomed out to nothing. I like the stability I am feeling now, and I don't want you to let it go!"

I replied, "I know you do not trust me, because of the past, and I understand why you don't. I will earn your trust and show you that I am listening to you and taking care of your needs. I will do whatever it takes to earn your trust, for I do love you and you matter. What you have to say is very important."

I received an interesting, yet challenging request from this little anxious one.

"I need you to promise you will call your friends tomorrow and let them know you are looking for work in Albuquerque and that you will continue listening to your inner guidance. I need you to act on your hunches immediately," the little anxious one demanded.

I agreed to do exactly that, feeling a true sense of supporting myself in a way far greater than I had ever experienced. I was listening to my inner needs and truly caring for myself. I understood now that I was living with an aspect of myself that distrusted me. This awareness gave me a feeling of being nurtured and cared for, something I had always looked for outside of myself, either from my parents or from my friends, and particularly from my intimate relationships.

It was interesting that many of my intimate relationships reflected the lack of caring about my needs, just as I had been disregarding them myself. When I did receive caring and love from my friends, however, I found it difficult to comprehend why these people would do so much for me. I was overcome with guilt. I asked myself questions like, "What do I possibly give to my friends that inspires them to give so much to me?" I was so out of touch with caring for myself by listening to and acting on my inner needs that it was difficult to accept my friends' caring and love, yet I longed for it. I had grown so tired of my feelings of guilt and unworthiness.

As I promised my little anxious one, I eagerly made my phone calls the next day, intending not only to find a position in Albuquerque, but more importantly, to prove to myself I could be trusted to take care of myself however I deemed appropriate.

I was determined to follow my intuition and take only the action I felt strongly about. I didn't feel like pouring myself all over the city, only to meet up with many dead ends, so I trusted my inner guidance. I recognized right action by the good feelings I had when thoughts came up of where I could go and who I could talk to about finding a new position.

That is exactly what happened one morning just a week or so after starting my process. I had an idea to visit a friend and discuss what was happening in Albuquerque, as I had been very out of touch for a long while. Oddly enough, I left that visit with a position in that company! They weren't actively looking for someone to fill the position I was offered; however, the situation was perfect for all of us. I sensed another beautiful miracle had happened in my life. I trusted in the power behind all things and surrendered to the flow regarding how things would actually materialize. Again, I just knew what I wanted, and I opened myself to that or something better. Could it be that I would never doubt again? I had a renewed sense of faith and trust in the "creative process."

I was truly enjoying my experience of stability and my sense of being grounded as a result of communicating with my feelings. I listened to my beliefs and the emotions that each had to offer, and I gave up my pattern of resistance to them. My inner feelings were no longer enemies; in fact, they had become pieces of a mystery that was somehow unfolding in my life—a mystery which seemed to leave me with a greater sense of love and acceptance for myself and others. I became more in touch with my true feelings and I validated them without resistance.

As if by magic, the attention to my feelings, expressed with understanding and compassion, seemed to leave me with a freedom and sense of power I had never known before. I was free to decide what I wanted to create from a place of delight and love, unlike the emotional attachments which satisfied old, denied, unmet needs, which were crying for love and attention. I was experiencing love as a healing power in a very personal way.

All Things Are Possible

I began paying closer attention to what I wanted while increasing my permission to have it. I came to realize it was me all along who was pushing away my desires with my resistant patterns of doubt, worry, and fear. I was learning to trust that God would lovingly fulfill my desires by materializing them with love. I was also realizing that I was the one who was closing the doors to receiving my desires by believing in my own unworthiness. I had been harboring feelings of guilt and shame for asking in the first place! I was beginning to get it. I knew I needed to first identify what I wanted in my heart. Once I was committed to having my desire, God would show me how it would come to fruition in the best possible way with the least amount of resistance.

"Perhaps now I am ready to open up to the idea of allowing the man of my dreams to come into my life and have the relationship that I've never before experienced," I thought with renewed anticipation. It was Christmas Day and I had a call from my dear friend and one of the greatest supporters of my creative endeavors, Bev. "Judy, what are two gorgeous women doing alone again on Christmas Day, when for the past three years we have wanted to be in loving, committed relationships?" she asked in a voice of determination and bewilderment. With a feeling of confusion, yet a renewed sense of determination, I agreed.

"What do you say we go for a hike and find a place to meditate and create these guys once and for all?" she responded. The continued strength in her voice echoed her conviction. We dressed warmly for our midday hike and off we went to the foothills of the beautiful Sandia Mountains, each of us carrying ourselves as if we were women with a mission. We radiated with a glow as if we had just been given the genie in the bottle and the magic was sure to be ours!

We began our hike down a well-trod path. Bev liked adventure, though, and soon she was leading us into a narrow riverbed, covered by Russian Olive and Pinon trees, Chamisa, and grasses native to our area. Up toward the mountain we hiked. Thirty minutes went by. We were filled with an anxious sense that something very definite was about to happen. We walked and walked through the thick brush when suddenly, in an open clearing, there it was: a beautiful, large, flat rock lying solid and smooth on the ground. We sensed it calling us.

We approached the rock, which was just large enough for the two of us to sit back to back, and we absorbed ourselves in the midday sun as if we were two lizards about to bask in the rays, nurtured by the heat and relaxed by the magic we both felt surrounding us in that spot.

As we positioned ourselves comfortably, we acknowledged, with a sense of certainty, just exactly what we were about to visualize. We agreed to let our imaginations run wild, just like the freedom we found in the mountains, not touched or manipulated by human hands, just the free-flowing power of nature majestically and abundantly endowing the land with magnificence. I felt somehow I had placed myself before the sacred altar of the Almighty Creator. A sense of reverence and stately power engulfed us as we summoned all the heavenly guides and angels to assist us in the creation of the two men we each had envisioned and talked about so many times before.

Time had passed beyond what it seemed, as we each came out of our meditation, feeling as if we had transported ourselves into the future. We discovered we had taken similar journeys in our minds. As we sat still and very quiet for a brief moment, chills permeated our bodies and a sense of completeness came over us simultaneously. We knew, unlike ever before, that we had been heard and we were ready to receive.

Slowly we rose and began our journey home, certain that our message of what we wanted in relationships was received by the universe and already existed. Our work was to be certain we were ready to receive what we had envisioned. Suddenly Bev asked me, "Judy, do you believe this man really does exist for you?" Then a thought struck me for the first time. I really did believe that the man I desired did actually exist for me, someone who honored his spiritual nature as well as his physical nature and who would walk through problems with me to the other side, rather than pretend that there were no problems and avoid them.

I realized that my belief that men would not look inward at themselves and feel their pain and grow from it had kept me in doubt all this time. I finally got it. What I wanted to attract was possible! I had never believed that the relationship I wanted could materialize for me because I truly didn't believe it was possible. Wow! It had been me all this time keeping what I so dearly wanted from myself because I doubted that there were infinite options in the universe.

I also realized that I believed what I wanted was too much for God! "You know, Bev, it's really true. What we think we know intellectually will not alter our life until we become aware of our resistant beliefs, make peace with them, and then release ourselves from them. I no longer believe that the man of my dreams can't exist, just because I've not seen him before. I'm open to new references for men!" I shouted with great conviction.

I saw the lie in my old belief that the type of man I wanted didn't exist. Why could I now believe that he did? What so convincingly shifted my perception? Why was I now at peace with the idea of having what I wanted without the nagging thought that he didn't exist, and if he did, he surely wouldn't be attracted to me? Something wonderfully healing had happened that allowed me to shift from what I thought were absolute truths to abandoning my old beliefs completely. I found myself feeling certain that I now had permission from all parts of myself to have what I wanted!

I knew I was experiencing the same level of certainty about manifesting this relationship as I had experienced when I knew my homes would sell in thirty days. My continued quest for the keys to become a master co-creator with the natural forces in the universe (I call God) intensified, for I knew my Beautiful Being was very present with me. The insights that came in the days ahead surged throughout my body and filled me with a sense of calm and peaceful knowing.

I had made a 100 percent shift in accepting myself, particularly regarding my body. I made a decision to love myself and to make peace with my body no matter what I weighed! I decided that if a man only wanted me if I looked perfect, then I wouldn't be interested in him. I wanted someone who valued heart and soul as well as the physical body. It is interesting how I had to value my heart and soul first before receiving the same feelings from someone else. It made sense that the Law of Attraction would, no doubt, bring this quality to me in a mate.

I conceded that my physical body is just too subject to change, and that maintaining the desire to control it is futile. I gave up the need to force my body into a mold that I thought would make me more lovable. I made peace with my body. Yes, I still chose to have a trim, healthy body; I just didn't need it to be that way for the purpose of trying to become more worthy and lovable. I wanted a healthy body for the purpose of honoring and loving me.

I knew that stopping the fight against my body and feeling love for it, while understanding that my extra weight was a result of me constantly focusing on and fearing that I wasn't desirable unless I looked perfect, was the primary action that cleared the way for a relationship to materialize in my life. As I held the idea in mind that my soul-mate relationship had already come to pass, I noticed an energy surging through my chest as the old, opposing thought patterns entered into my conscious mind.

"Men only want you for your body, and that is shameful. You will be used; what you want will never be as important as what a man wants." I relaxed into these sensations, telling myself, "This too shall pass. I now have new information." I knew the old thought forms were on their way out! I knew who was talking, and it wasn't me.

Within this process, I thanked the beliefs which stated that men are abusive. This was all based on my past experiences. I thanked my body, including the extra fifteen pounds, for reflecting the truth of my fears so they could be shed in the light of awareness and love. This, by the way, was also the beginning of shedding the extra fifteen pounds!

No longer did I need to affix my attention on what I did not want to happen, thinking that was the way to stop or eliminate it. I had a habit of staring at conditions I didn't want all the time, complaining about what I didn't want instead of talking about what I *did* want. I used to feel compelled to keep focused on my fears in urgent attempts to guard against them in order to keep them from eating me alive!

I couldn't look at them without pushing against them, feeling scared and angry all the while. Truly, I did give up the fight—the fight against what I didn't want, NOT the vision of what I wanted. Another valuable insight that created an opportunity for this relationship to occur was my willingness to remain single rather than settle for anything less than what I desired. I trusted myself to say "NO" to what I knew I didn't want rather than settling for less and trying to remold some poor soul into being someone else. I didn't HAVE to have a relationship anymore. I just wanted one, and I was free to choose it because of love and sharing, not for the purpose of bringing me security when I didn't feel secure or feeling wanted when I didn't feel wanted.

This soul-mate relationship was no longer needed as a remedy to fix what I originally thought was broken inside of me. I consciously felt the painful beliefs I had created so long ago, beliefs about needing my security to come from a man and not being worthy enough to be loved and wanted just for myself. By seeing these unconscious beliefs for what they really were, a perspective from a small child, and not fighting to get rid of them, not denying or avoiding them, just acknowledging I had them and feeling them fully, their power dissolved automatically.

This created a space for new possibilities and for my desire to be realized. I swept up all the energy I had sacrificed to fight and overcompensate for my negative patterns of beliefs and to hide the shame that plagued me for so long. I focused it all on my new loving relationship with the energy of creation behind it!

Chapter 8

My Soul Mate—
A "Magical" Attraction

Several days had gone by after my powerful walk with Bev when a thought occurred to me while at dinner with my daughter, Lori. "Lori, we are tuned in to each other so well, and you know about the man I really want. What if you pretend you can see him right here in front of us at this table. Tell me what he is wearing and how he looks to you." I chuckled. "Just play with the ideas that come into your head and have fun with them." I believed strongly in what she was about to say.

"Okay, Mom. I don't know if I can do it, but I'll try," she responded. Lori suddenly had a glazed look in her beautiful blue eyes as she stared out into space as if she were truly looking at someone.

"Well, he kind of has black and gray hair, like salt and pepper, real thick, and he has a mustache," she said with sincere conviction. "He's wearing a brown leather jacket, dark trousers; he's kind of GQish looking."

"What do you mean by GQish?" I responded with a puzzled look.

"Oh, you know, dressed really stylish and 'in' looking. He drives a car and I'm not sure what it is. Kind of like a Saab or something like that. No, not a Saab but like that," she said with the same tone of conviction as if she were looking right at the car!

"Wow, Lori." I gasped. "I feel the presence of who you just described as if he were here right now!" We looked at each other in amazement at how the description just flowed out of her.

A few weeks prior to this conversation with Lori and my visit to the rock with Bev, I had enrolled in a course based on the book *You Can Have It All*, by Arnold Patent. I enrolled in this class right after returning from Hawaii. It had piqued my interest, and the impulse to attend it carried increased enthusiasm for me. Upon the completion of the course, six weeks later, I experienced a subtle yet profound occurrence that truly changed my life!

One particular Sunday, after attending a service at the church where I belonged and where I had attended the classes, I was drawn to a gathering of people for refreshments afterwards. I noticed a

My Soul Mate—A "Magical" Attraction

man from my class whom I distinctly remembered having been drawn to. He caught my eye as if to invite a meeting. This came as quite a surprise to me, because when I first saw him in the class, I had decided that he definitely looked like he was married. He carried himself with a sense of sureness and stability. He appeared to be totally at peace with who he was. He seemed quite different from the prowling sort of guys I had grown so tired of.

I felt my heart pounding as he approached me and introduced himself again, as if he needed to refresh my memory that we had been in a class together! Of course I remembered him; not as a single guy, however! And, it turned out, he *was* single! We exchanged phone numbers and set a date for dinner the next week.

"The doorbell is ringing, Mom," Lori shouted from her room. I was so nervous my heart was racing as if this were my first date in high school. I took a gasping deep breath and opened the door to the most gentle, glowing face I had ever seen.

"Hi, Arny," I burst out with a smile. "Please come in and meet my daughter, Lori." I could see her look of eagerness as she approached the foyer. Then, suddenly, with what appeared to be déjà vu, Lori and I stared at each other in total awe. "Lori, do you remember the description you recited at dinner about two weeks ago of the man I had talked about meeting?" We were both incredulous. We starred at this poor man who didn't quite understand what was going on. Arny had salt-and-pepper hair, a mustache, dark brown leather jacket, and dark trousers. He was definitely GQish!

"How can this be?" I gasped. It's as if Lori saw right into the future of what had already been prepared. It was just like the feelings I had at the rock, knowing that what I had asked for was already complete as far as the universe was concerned. This was just a scene in the unfolding of it all. It was only Act I of many beautiful acts that have taken place since that day. We both knew, after a six-hour, nonstop-talking dinner date, we were each in front of the very one we had dreamed of, a perfect soul mate in every way.

One Monday morning, a couple of months after our magical first date, I received a red rose at my office from Arny. I thought, "Oh, how sweet!" Well, it didn't stop there. The next week I received two long-stemmed red roses, and again I thought, "How sweet!"

After the third week, and having received three red roses, I thought the same thing: "Oh, how sweet." My assistant, however, said to me, "Judy, don't you know what he is doing?" Well, I wish I could have said yes, but . . . not.

She said, "He has a plan. What do you think is going to happen in the twelfth week when he sends you a dozen long-stemmed red roses?" I was still clueless. No man had ever treated me like this before. She suggested to me that Arny's intention was to propose to me at the twelfth rose. "Right," I thought! I shrugged the idea off as a great one, although highly unlikely. Actually, it didn't take but a nanosecond for my old belief system to overtake my possibility thinking. No way!

After all of the inner work I had done, I still couldn't accept the fact that Arny was the one, that I was actually involved with "the one." Yet, as I say this, I did know that I knew; deep in my gut, I knew. Well, as one might have guessed, Arny's plan was to propose to me on Father's Day, which was twelve weeks from when the first rose arrived. Yet man makes plans and God laughs.

One evening, a week before Father's Day, we were having dinner in Santa Fe. It was magical. One thing led to another, and the conversation was conducive for what happened next. Arny suddenly excused himself—actually he bolted from the table—and when he returned, he had a little black box in his hand. I could feel an energy all around us. It was magical, it was palpable. The next thing I heard was Arny proposing to me in a rather surprisingly apologetic way. "Judy, I love you so much. Will you marry me? I know how particular you are. I thought you would want to have a say in picking out your engagement ring, so I bought you these earrings. I couldn't propose to you without offering you something beautiful to wear from me."

I couldn't fight back the tears. I felt my chest pounding. I couldn't believe what had just happened. Actually, I don't think Arny could either. We both tried hard to capture this special moment, knowing it would have to come to an end. It was just so perfect, so sweet, so what I had been dreaming of for so long. My head continued to spin as I tried to assimilate and believe in what had just happened.

He said, "I have had these earrings in my car for a couple of weeks. I intended to propose to you on Father's Day." It was one week before, yet the timing was perfect, as we both knew. Of course I said, "Yes!"

I was awe-struck at how dramatically my life had turned around exactly as I intended, even better! Arny and I planned a trip to San Diego soon after Father's Day. Our flight was reserved, our plans were made. At the last minute, air travel went berserk. Our flight to San Diego was cancelled. We changed our plans and decided to go to San Francisco instead. Fortunately, we were able to book a flight with no problem.

Off we went, excited and so in love. What I didn't realize at the time was that I was about to live out a scene that I had been visualizing in my imagination for almost two years. In my mental scene, I was with the man of my dreams in a swanky restaurant in San Francisco. I saw an image of a room filled with tables that were dressed with white linen tablecloths. They provided a classy backdrop for the candles that adorned each table. I imagined that this restaurant was on the second floor of a building in Union Square. It had tall windows that reached from the floor to the ceiling. I saw my ideal man and me sitting at one of the tables. He was reaching into his suit coat pocket, pulling out a sweet little box, and presenting me with an engagement ring.

I had imagined for so long that my ideal mate, the love of my life, would offer me this beautiful ring and say to me adoringly, "Judy, I love you so much. I want to spend the rest of my life with you. Will you accept this ring and marry me?" Déjà vu! It hit me. I felt like I was in a bubble lost in time. I had to step back for a moment and maintain my composure. Yes, I was stunned! This moment was playing out exactly as I had envisioned it, over and over again. I was so taken aback by this experience.

While Arny had already officially proposed to me a few weeks before, this was the dream I had seen for so long. This very moment, straight out of my imagination, was playing itself out in real life, the dream I had felt and imagined for two years. There we were, in San Francisco, in the restaurant that I had imagined, with the man of my dreams professing his undying love for me, adoring me, and wanting me in his life forever. Whew! That was a lot to take in.

And, to be consistent with my dream, Arny did reach into his coat pocket in that swanky San Francisco restaurant and pull out a beautiful diamond engagement ring that he and I had designed together. I still relish that story to this day. This was a shining example of what is truly possible with the creative power that I had learned to access and consciously rely upon.

My past did not set me up to have this kind of experience, this kind of love and commitment. Yet, because of my inner work, I changed my deepest mind about what was possible for me. I transformed the idea of who I thought I was into the truth: I am a powerful creator, a woman who deserves to be loved unconditionally, someone who possesses the capacity to trust, to be loved, and to love a man unconditionally. That was a miracle. And it just happened for me!

Nearly a year later, Bev and I each married the men we dreamed of at the rock. We were engaged one week apart and married two weeks apart. Everything fell together for her as perfectly as it did for me. We knew in our hearts, with absolute conviction, that the unions we each experienced were meant to be.

It was clear to me by now that most of the visions I had seen for myself while I was still living in Santa Fe had at last come to pass. I had built a strong belief and faith in my ability to take control of my life and actually bring about the changes I wanted, not merely a different set of challenging circumstances that reflected the same old patterns.

After multiple failed marriages, it was a major accomplishment to know I had at last dissolved the negative, fearful, and limited patterns of my past. Making peace with my opposing negative beliefs and taking back my authority and power was the only way I could change the course of my life in such a miraculous way.

Chapter 9

The Impossible Dream Comes True

My dreams were coming true at last. I felt like Cinderella and as if the midnight hour would never come. The stroke of midnight that would turn it all back to darkness had passed me by. My understanding of the incredible laws of the universe brought me a sense of security that I knew I could always depend on. I knew that I could make decisions and choices for myself and that the loving source of all things would bring about my desires, in the perfect time, for the highest good of all concerned. My work was to be willing to release the opposing, doubtful thought patterns while I focused on what I wanted. I realized, however, that my soul's intentions for growth and the expansion of love would always bring me another opportunity that would accomplish just that, more growth and love. My IRS debt was about to fulfill that very intention.

As Arny and I began our beautiful life together, many changes became evident. The apartment that Lori and I were living in would not serve the needs of our blended family. Arny and I began creating ideas for our new home together. Our plans involved selling his home, too. It became clear to me that the heavy cloud of my IRS debt, which had grown to out-of-sight proportions, had to finally be resolved.

Throughout the years, I had remained most cooperative with the IRS, thanks to my dear friend and CPA, Bill. His ability to work with and respond to this giant entity guided me in times when I felt most oppressed by the ever-increasing debt. My income had been reduced drastically since the sale of my business and my divorce. The very idea of satisfying this debt seemed so impossible, I could hardly think about it without panicking. Well, it was time to start thinking about it in ways that would resolve the matter. I could not run from it anymore.

At first, I overwhelmed myself with questions like, "How will I ever be rid of this debt?" I ruminated over this unresolved question to the point of exhaustion. Feelings of sheer panic and anger haunted me as I faced what I perceived to be an unavoidable disaster from my previous divorce. As I brought this dragon to the forefront of my life, the buried, seething, fearful feelings came forward, too. "Could I possibly imagine myself free from this one?" I dared to ask myself.

I remembered that the great laws of the universe never fail. My Beautiful Inner Being was most definitely with me, and I understood how to manifest better than ever before. This truly tested my faith; however, I had nothing to lose and everything to gain. I drew upon my faith to help me believe that this unbelievable situation could and would be resolved. I just had no idea how!

I began slowly and tentatively visualizing a paid debt. At first, feelings and sensations of hopelessness and panic surged through my body, opposition and doubt screaming, "Have you gone mad?" I continued loving those parts of myself, not knowing how this out-of-control situation could ever be resolved. Slowly I imagined faint pictures of a paid debt as clearly as my doubting mind would allow. My faith in the creative process brought me peace and hope once again.

Months had gone by when, one day, I received a phone call from Bill. He was excited and hopeful because he had just learned of an opportunity that could potentially save me from financial ruin. The IRS had decided to compromise old tax debts in certain circumstances. It appeared that mine could be one of those circumstances. Due to the brilliant strategies that Bill implemented on my behalf, I was granted such a compromise. The debt was reduced to an amount I could easily pay, ten cents on the dollar. Now, that was a miracle!

My cooperation and belief in God's universal laws and love paid off once again. All things are truly possible with divine love!

Conclusions—
Part I

You have just completed a journey that took me years to live and to learn from. That, I think, is the beauty of learning from the wisdom of others. I have opened the door of my life and invited you in for the purpose of helping you to see what is possible. Through understanding how the Law of Attraction works and trusting in the mighty power of unconditional love, you too can deliberately create your life to reflect your truest desires.

My experience in the business world for the past forty years has taught me how to achieve success by setting goals and defining a plan of action. This approach has served me and many others quite well; however, I have also observed many inconsistencies in just relying on this external approach to successfully achieve what you want both in business and in personal life. Why? The answers are actually revealed throughout my story. I shared many examples that mirrored back my inner conflicts and resistance. My internal conflict shattered many of my significant goals, dreams, and desires. My intention is to keep this from happening to you.

The idea of conflict within yourself may not be new to you. What keeps this conflict ongoing, however, depends upon your attitude toward your conflict and the subsequent manner in which you handle it. This can make the difference between realizing your heart's desires or not.

I was blessed to have discovered a healing process that I call Alchemy of the Shadow. It came to me one night when I was very distraught as I reflected on my very pathetic life, or so I felt. I pondered how it could be that everything in my life was what I didn't want. I hated my life and I felt so ashamed to face my reality. It was the night I met my little angry one face to face.

I spoke about this in my story in Chapter three. If you recall, I went into a meditative trance and met my anger head-on. In my attempt to forgive my mother and father, I felt a lot of resistance to the idea. Through the healing process of Alchemy of the Shadow, I discovered why I couldn't forgive them and the part my anger played in it all.

Alchemy of the Shadow will literally elevate you out of your internal conflicts and your negative, hidden, protective beliefs and emotions. You will come to see the brilliant truth of who you really are as your authentic, loving, and powerful self. I discovered that this very essential step, my alchemy process, must be included in the art of conscious manifesting if you want to realize your desires and your dreams. This was a step I hadn't ever realized. Unknowingly, I was resisting my internal resistance. Worse yet, it felt like the right thing to do! It created a blind spot for me. I couldn't see that my resistance was the problem.

Alchemy of the Shadow is a method that will help you ascend out of your fearful, guarded, resistant survival system. When you connect with your authentic self, you will experience your life in a much more loving, joyful, enthusiastic, and expanded way. Your authentic magical self is the vibrational essence from which your dreams and desires are made and from which they materialize.

In Part II of this book, I detail this process and guide you through the essential steps that are so often missed in the art of conscious manifesting. I share the exact steps that will assist you in experiencing your own Alchemy of the Shadow so you too can thrive and create the extraordinary life you were born to live! My intention is for you to experience your greatest life and creative expression from your greatest self.

I invite you to give yourself the gift of utilizing this beautiful, effective process, one that I attest has turned my life around. I am so pleased to say that it has also turned around the lives of hundreds of others I have taught it to.

Become an alchemist and turn your life (ordinary metal) into your dreams (gold). Begin it now. Come with me, and let's create your life by design from your true authentic, creative, and powerful self!

Part II

How to Ascend Out of Your Survival System and Miraculously Transform Your Life

Your Survival System— Fight-Flight-Freeze

My life reflected a complete turnaround from the depths of despair and hopelessness to the heights of joy and ecstasy. The fact that I finally brought the results I wanted into my life with peace, gentleness, and ease was truly a miracle. The struggle and fight that I experienced for so many years came from my threatening negative beliefs which triggered my automatic reactive survival system. When unexpected and difficult things happened to me, I unconsciously reacted from my survival patterns. Sadly, I didn't know there could be a better way. Unfortunately, the fact that I was unaware of spending so much of my early life reacting to difficult situations and people from my fight-flight-freeze responses didn't give me immunity from experiencing the detrimental consequences that occurred over and over again.

Your Oldest Reptilian Brain

Your fight-flight-freeze reactions come from the oldest part of your brain. This primitive brain is in charge of your basic and oldest survival concerns; that is, kill or be killed, eat or be eaten, control or be controlled, etc. Actually, this describes how I approached so much of my early life. And, from my observations in dealing with others, it appeared to me that so many other people were also living their lives from their fearful habit patterns. This made my world all the more terrifying.

The fact is, our ancestors had to run from saber-toothed tigers and hunt for their food. Basic survival was their primary concern. This part of the human brain did, in fact, ensure the continuation of the human species. Our ancestors weren't wiped out by the saber-toothed tigers, thus we are still here today!

Unfortunately, many of us in today's modern world are still operating from our automatic fight-flight-freeze patterns on a daily basis. We are allowing these stress patterns to take charge of

Your Survival System—Fight-Flight-Freeze

our lives and blaming everything else for the havoc they cause. We don't have to run from the saber-toothed tigers; however, we're now running from competition or we're trying to beat it. We are not hunting for food in the wild; we're hunting for jobs to pay for our food, often in frantic and hostile emotional environments.

Approaching life's challenges from your survival system is dangerous to your health and emotional well-being, odd as that may seem. This part of your brain is technically called your sympathetic nervous system. It is designed to protect you when you perceive there is a threat. If you operate from it as a daily practice, however, it will make you sick, broke, and alone. That's what eventually happened to me.

My saving grace was that I was fortunate enough to have been blessed with discovering a way in which I could function from a higher, more effective part of myself. This magical place within me was where I connected with my divine creative power. I literally turned my life around. I believe that once you take the quantum leap to experience your higher, most effective and creative self, it will make the difference between heaven and hell on earth for you, too!

So, would you like to gain access to this higher place within you? And do you wonder how it will affect your daily life once you do connect? Will your conscious connection to your personal greater power bring you what you truly want in your life, like more money, optimum health, a true sense of well-being, your soul mate, happiness, fulfillment, joy and love? The answer is most definitely a resounding, "Yes, it is all possible for YOU!"

You are here to create what matters to you most. I'm offering you the key that will open the door to your freedom and power, a power that transcends the need to force things to happen, to struggle with what is or isn't. By connecting with your authentic creative power, you will stop the suffering that occurs when you *resist* what isn't working in any area of your life.

You are designed to bring about your deepest, most sincere desires easily and effortlessly. This requires that you leap into a new vibrational dimension within yourself, if you will. I am not suggesting that you just adopt a new set of conscious beliefs or heady affirmations that you say over and over to yourself. I am talking about accessing a completely different emotional and spiritual realm that is within you, and you do this through the art of nonresistance.

My experiences within the depths of despair and depression, a depression that caused me to entertain death as a far better choice than living, were urgent enough to send me on my insatiable quest for peace and positive changes in my life. I became obsessed in seeking the answer for one puzzling question, "What happened that destroyed my life and how can I turn it all around?" Everything seemed fine and then suddenly, BOOM, the bottom fell out of everything. One thing I did come to realize was that my relationship to God as my power, my source, and my everything, had to change completely! I just needed to know how to do that.

God—the Santa Claus Syndrome

Messages from many illuminated masters and great teachers have come before us to enlighten us with the truth of who we really are and what we are capable of achieving. So often, I believe, these masters have been misinterpreted by our fear. The "God" many people (myself included) have come to know through well-intentioned religious organizations sits on the throne in heaven somewhere out there, critically judges us, and disapprovingly looks down upon us. This idea of God is being portrayed as completely separate from us by many religions and has been for thousands of years.

My desperate need to feel connected to a God that I could believe would unconditionally love me just the way I am is what drove my insatiable quest for love and connection for years. I became so confused as I attempted to learn and to obey God's rules as the different religions presented them. Each religion claimed to possess the right rules, of course. I discovered there were as many rules as there were religions.

My initial exposure to God was like the Santa Claus Syndrome— good little boys and girls get the goodies, while bad little boys and girls get none. A sense of being controlled by the one with the goodies left me feeling fearful and shamefully inferior. I felt subjugated by the judgment of how well "Santa Claus"— in other words, God—thought I had behaved. As children, many of us (I for one) looked to our parents and authority figures the same way.

Not only has the notion of being left out of the goodies (heaven) been the warning, even worse, we will be punished forever (hell) if we fail to obey. This notion increased my fear level well beyond that of my emotional tolerance.

So, what can you do? You can either fixate on pleasing or being good (flight) or you can rebel against the rules and eliminate the notion that there is a God (fight) altogether. Or, better yet, you can discover what I did. There is a loving, benevolent God that knows you, that unconditionally loves you just the way you are and just the way you are not, a God who wants you to experience the authentic you, is never separate from you, and desires for you to know what unconditional love and forgiveness are really all about. You are a powerful creator. You are so much greater than what your survival self can see and experience.

One thing is certain. Being driven by your survival patterns can only produce results that may help you temporarily feel better about yourself or feel safe. Once the outer conditions that you think you need to feel okay in the world go away, you'll be right back in your fearful state of anxiety, fear, panic, and doubt. The good news is, there is a better way. . .

Neutral Awareness—Your First Step to Freedom

The first step toward making the long-term changes that produce the results and outcomes that you prefer is to:

- become aware of your emotional survival patterns
- discover your deep, limiting stories about yourself and your world
- discover the meaning that is associated with what is hap-pen-ing around you
- do this without judgment and resistance.

Within the essential first step of awareness, you must suspend the need to change anything and everything! **This is the simplest, yet most difficult thing to do—to have awareness without judgment and resistance.**

You must feel the truth about where you are and feel it deeply in your body. You will know if you are in your survival realm if you feel threatened and fearful, and if you have a heightened sense of urgency to do something. If you are in your highly functioning power place, you will notice that you feel centered, present, and resourceful, particularly when unexpected adversities or difficult people show up.

Distinguishing Your Survival System

One sure way to distinguish between your survival system and your higher vibrational realm can be in taking note of your emotions and your subsequent behaviors that are driven by your emotions. If you feel threatened and become resentful or angry, you will likely notice that your attention gets hijacked away from the present moment. You will become fixated on eliminating or guarding against (fighting) what you perceive is threatening you. Often this takes on the form of blaming or controlling others and needing to be right.

Resistance to fear has a way of causing avoidance and denial (flight). You might procrastinate taking actions that would bring about positive changes. It is easy to practice denial by suppressing your emotions, toughening up, and ignoring your needs, often in favor of others' needs. The hidden beliefs that fuel your fear show up in your head as the mean and hurtful voices that suggest you are inferior, less than, not good enough, etc.

If you are trapped in shame or guilt, you will discover yourself withdrawing from others or feeling resigned about anything changing for the better. All of this energy-draining activity is a clue that you are functioning out of your old survival brain and that you are viewing life from the victim perspective. Unfortunately, you won't have access to your objective, reasoning mind or your imagination. You will not be able to entertain new possibilities and creative solutions to your problems.

Worse yet, your communication and behavior with others will be driven by your own personal need to get out of pain, an emotional pain that you subconsciously believe you can't handle. Others will appear to you as the enemy or they'll seem like obstacles that are interfering with what you need. It is also possible that you'll see others as a means to meet a need that you have. They will appear to you as objects, just a means to an end. You will be self-centered, yet you'll feel justified in your harmful, defensive behaviors. You can't help any of this if you are being unconsciously run by your survival brain.

Stressed-out humans are driven on a daily basis by their survival-oriented sympathetic nervous system. Our survival brain is predominantly wired to look out for danger and to be safe and secure. Unfortunately, this objective overrides our ability to create something better and new. We cannot be the co-creators we were designed to be when we identify as victims and react from our survival perspective.

The Two Sides of Fear

Seeking a true sense of well-being, of being accepted and loved and being safe and protected, is the root desire beneath all this primitive brain activity. Think about it for yourself. If you must control people and your environment, aren't you afraid something bad will happen to you or someone you love? Or perhaps you fear you won't get something you really believe you must have to feel secure. You might be overcontrolling your children, your body, your finances, your partner or spouse.

My attempts to control my body through crazy food addictions only made me crazier. My continued resistance to not looking "perfect," whatever that meant, kept me spinning around in circles, miserable and very alone. Yet at the time, I believed being perfect would win "the guy." It did win the guys—just all the wrong ones.

Are you being driven by your survival system? Is stress ruling your life? Does your motivation to act often come from fear or anger? If your answer to these questions is yes, you probably do feel as if you are being chased by the tigers in life (flight), the tigers being controlling people or negative circumstances, as in not having enough money or love, etc.

You might notice yourself "in flight" the next time you go out of your way to please someone at your own expense. Do your physical or economic conditions have to get so bad before you will make a move to change, just as mine did when I was finally so broke I was forced back to work and had to swallow my pride?

Perhaps you've played the other side of the "fear coin" and have overpowered people with force (fight). You became the tiger yourself. Have you ever withdrawn your acceptance of people when they disagreed with you? Maybe you've pushed yourself to work harder when you were tired and ignored your feelings when you felt hurt.

Both sides of this fear coin are designed to avoid difficult feelings like fear, shame, separation, and a sense of powerlessness (tails), at the same time you seek to feel powerful and "good enough" (heads). There is no way to resolve your conflict within this win/lose system. Why? Because it is fueled by your unconscious resistance, and that is what keeps your inner conflict going. And that's the problem, resistance.

Resistance—What You Resist Persists!

There are long-term consequences of not paying attention when your hot buttons get pushed and your subsequent reactions ensue. There is a universal Law of Attraction which states that "like attracts like." It will always bring you what you subconsciously believe. This is very important to remember! This law never stops working. It responds to your subconscious, emotional (vibrational) mind, not your conscious thinking, desires, or actions.

What does this mean? Your subconscious mind is always thinking and feeling according to what you believe deeply; therefore you are always attracting. You will attract what you subconsciously and habitually think about, not what you consciously say you want. As funny as this may sound, your subconscious mind thinks for you, especially when you are not paying attention or being in the present moment.

When your basic core identity is aligned with a victim perspective of powerlessness and you continue to act from resistance, fear, anger, guilt, and shame, you will attract more circumstances and people into your life that will magnify these difficult emotions as well as deepen your identity as a victim. My story was filled with lots of evidence of this truth. I discovered, often the hard way, that you cannot fool Mother Nature by hiding from what you subconsciously believe by attempting to override it or to pretend otherwise.

Success, growth, and happiness ultimately occur as a result of you being willing to accept and interrupt these fearful, subconscious survival patterns. Only then can you introduce new ideas and perspectives that are aligned with love and divine creative power, perspectives that see the truth of who you truly are. This is what conscious awakening is all about.

During the time when I longed to feel secure and prosperous, I focused on being in Hawaii, yet I felt desperate, frustrated, and angry with the circumstances I was in. Do you remember how miserable and off base I was in Hawaii? I did not change my attitude and cease my resistance toward my current circumstances before I left for Hawaii; therefore, I attracted experiences in Hawaii that magnified my feelings of fear, loneliness, and desperation. My resistance persisted.

Your Survival Patterns—Your Body

There's more to this survival story. Your physical body is also impacted. While you are operating in the fight-or-flight mode, your body produces survival hormones, adrenaline and cortisol. When released into your bloodstream, these hormones shift fat molecules into your abdominal region. Your body gets prepared to run or to fight for your physical survival! This creates the infamous muffin top that so many of us work frantically to get rid of. Ironic, isn't it, that the more stress we have about our muffin-top bellies, the more we perpetuate our muffin tops.

If you suffered trauma or abuse as a child and you continue to deny your difficult emotions to avoid the hurt and pain, please consider that the constant stress from your unresolved inner conflict could be hanging out around your stomach.

The cellular programming that infuses your body with temporary surges of energy whenever you perceive that you or someone you care about is in danger is your body's brilliant design to meet the physical demands it thinks you have. Running or fighting, however, does not resolve the problem, the source of your emotional fears. Emotional fear comes from your negative subconscious belief patterns. Your beliefs subsequently become the source of your life experiences.

Your beliefs will continue to produce evidence in your life that proves them right. Not because they are the absolute truth, but because this is the way your subconscious mind works. Unfortunately, this deepens your conviction for your beliefs, and on and on it goes. It goes on until you stop it. And you *can* stop it and change it. Alchemy of the Shadow will help you to do just that.

For the longest time, I arranged my life to avoid pain and seek pleasure. I experienced cravings for more money, job security, the perfect body, my ideal mate, and I needed to maintain a lifestyle that was designed to impress others to make me "look good enough." These futile attempts to fulfill my unmet needs and to overcome the shame of who I thought I was only created havoc in my life. This is what threw me into my five-year "dark night of the soul." I lost all of what I needed to keep the dramatic façade going. Thank God for that!

My life was filled with excessive activity: I shopped when I felt insecure; I ate when I felt scared and alone; and I worked excessively long, hard hours to try to maintain control of the impressive world I had built up around me. All of this crazy activity was my urgent attempt to feel good enough, to be accepted, and to feel safe in my inner world of chaos.

I have described what happens when you are overtaken by your primitive survival system. It is not until you truly understand that it can never accomplish what you really want and need, that you will be able to let it go and ascend into your authentic powerful self. You will come to see that there is a better way to live, a way that inspires you to act from your soul's passion and purpose, to live from a higher truth about who you really are and what you're really capable of achieving without the stress and conflict that you may be living now.

This is the beginning point from which deliberate creating takes place. You will come to understand and consciously accept what your inner conflict and resistance is trying to do for you. Through the process of Alchemy of the Shadow, your life-force energy will be freed up; you'll trust and willingly give up the fight. Then and only then can you redirect your energy and attention toward your desires.

When I decided I wanted to be in a committed relationship and a subconscious part of me resisted the idea because of my painful past, my result was no relationship. Through Alchemy of the Shadow, I was free and safe to give myself permission to allow my soul mate to come into my life. And voilà, my soul mate appeared!

Contrast—Conflict—Resistance: Oh My!

Throughout my many years of seeking ways to turn my life around, I studied methods of success that boldly suggested that I get rid of my subconscious negative beliefs. This "getting rid of" attitude perpetuated the hostile environment I already had within me. I thought everything about me was wrong. Furthermore, I believed I had to get rid of the bad parts of myself in order to have the life I dreamed of. This attitude of getting rid of a part of me triggered more hostile reactions within me. My internal survival self pushed back and resisted all of my attempts to change.

It does seem logical to get rid of things that don't work, right? However, if you have been trying to get rid of your negative beliefs or behaviors, those aspects within you that you feel are unacceptable, and if you have not been successful in doing so, there is a very sound reason why your attempts have failed. It's not your fault.

It's true that your fearful beliefs trigger your survival patterns and they prevent you from attaining what you want in your life. However, **it is your negative reaction to these beliefs and behaviors** that perpetuate the very conditions you are so determined to get rid of! If you react to yourself or your outer world by blaming, judging, or complaining, you will perpetuate your negative experiences and feelings. Fighting against what you don't want, whether it's internal or external, will attract more of what you are trying to get rid of. This can only be expected due to the Law of Attraction. My continued anger and blame attracted more and more situations that reflected and magnified my fear and anger.

Think about it this way. Where is your focus and energy directed when you perceive something is coming at you full force? Would you not be on guard, watching every move it made? I was angry and frustrated as I blamed and complained about the distressing financial state and lonely conditions I was in during my dark hours of depression. I reacted as though these conditions had a mind of their own and were against me. I felt like a victim to my inner negative beliefs and to my outer needy circumstances.

The more I studied successful, caring, and fearless leaders and role models, the more intense and awful my life appeared to me. My contrast was so great! I didn't realize, during that time, how important it was to make peace with the survival beliefs and behaviors that were the source of my misery. I just hated it all. I seriously needed for my inner conflicts and desperate feelings to go away.

Unwanted conditions or difficult people are NOT technically against you. And the fact that they show up in your life does not mean there is something inherently wrong with you. They are just results that your subconscious beliefs produce, the beliefs and meanings that you concluded as a very young child.

The Origin of Your Symbiotic Survival Pattern—Fight-and-Flight Twins

Here's how it all began. Between the ages from birth to about 7 years old, if you were exposed to highly stressful, emotional, confusing, hurtful, or abusive environments, your little mind tried to make sense of your world to feel safe and secure. You made up reasons why your parents, teachers, schoolmates and others did hurtful things to you, or failed to meet your basic needs to feel loved, accepted, and protected. For sanity's sake, you most likely made yourself wrong rather than live with the fact that your parents or caregivers were incapable of giving you what you emotionally or physically needed.

It was just too scary a notion that your parents were inadequate to give you what you needed. Instead, you most likely told yourself something like, "I'm bad," or "I'm a loser," "I'm not _____ enough," or "I don't matter." Your mistreatment made sense to you. You concluded that you were being mistreated, left, ignored, punished, or consistently yelled at because you were a bad person, stupid, or wrong at the core, etc.

Your mind had a new agenda; enter your symbiotic twin. Your "fighter" twin's job was to save you by figuring out how to make you better by being more perfect, smarter, stronger, or judgmental and critical, and so on. This character might have even felt the need to resist and numb your hurtful or shameful feelings. Your negative feelings existed as a result of the negative conclusions you made about yourself in an attempt to bring sanity into your little world.

You actually had two survival characters making up one pattern. You couldn't have one without the other. Unfortunately, because of resistance, one character just reinforced the other. One side of this survival pattern was needed to overcompensate for and shut out the other side that felt unloved, unaccepted, and powerless. Your survival mind compelled your "fighter" character to be vigilant in its quest to strive to make you better and stronger so you could be safe, loved, and accepted. All of this was at the cost of you accepting yourself just as you were. **This is your inner conflict.**

And now, here you are today. You are waking up to this vigilant, futile quest that is still trying to get you what you needed as a little child, a quest that has been fueled by a lie all along. A lie that came from your very little self who made up a story that you were to blame for the inadequacies of your parents or caregivers. Thus what you perceived as a justified self-image and a victim identity followed you throughout your life.

It was NOT your doing that you were exposed to the environment that you were raised in. And it was NOT your fault that your brain was a sponge and soaked up any and all of the negative energy and teachings that you learned from your parents or caregivers. Yet your brain was programmed accordingly. None of this was your fault. However, it is now your responsibility and your right to change it, and you can!

So if you know that you are fighting against and hating what is inside of you or what is inside of others, please remember that while your past programming was not your fault, the consequences of your past programming will continue to bring about your greatest fears. You will attract what you fear and hate until you change your mind about who you are and what you are truly capable of. Now, let's use this understanding to help you change and get what you want with grace and ease.

Important Keys to Enter into Your Creative Kingdom

Remember my stories about selling my homes in 30 days regardless of the market? I discovered some very important distinctions that are a must when you want to cooperate with the Law of Attraction and create what you want or something better.

- **Feel immense love and appreciation:** I felt so much love for the homes I created. Yes, I had decided to sell them. They weren't serving me and my family anymore. We had outgrown them, just as you have outgrown your protective, fearful beliefs. My vision of what I wanted going forward in my life had changed. Did I curse my homes, disgusted that they were no longer serving me? Did I want to burn them down or leave them abruptly in anger to get rid of them? No. I loved them and appreciated how well they had served me. While this sounds a bit dramatic, it is true. Appreciating your current inner survival reality for the gifts it has brought you up to this point in your life can be challenging; yet it is a key to freedom into your inner creative kingdom.
- **Make peace with the worst-case scenario:** I did have to make peace with the possibility that my homes might not have sold. I had to accept that I could live with the worst-case scenario that I thought could happen. This allowed me to let go of the idea that my homes had to sell. Any threatening ideas that suggested something horrible might happen if they didn't sell and that I couldn't live with it had to be released. Had I sent fear messages to my brain, I would have triggered chaos in my world. Resistance, doubt, and fear would have closed off any possibility for miracles to happen.
- **Let go of the panic and urgency:** As I let go of the threatening idea that my homes had to sell or else I would die, a sense of relief came over me. My fear and panic dissolved. I

easily dismissed any threatening stories that my fearful mind could conjure up. I dissolved the urgency to hurry up and make something happen. The result: my homes always sold in 30 days for just the right price and in markets and price ranges that typically were not selling.

A good description for the process of giving up and surrendering your fight is letting go—letting go of the resistance and the fight, not of your desires. I have come to realize a very important fact. We are not called to stop wanting our pleasures and desires. **We are, however, called to stop using our desires as a remedy or a cover-up for our subconscious negative beliefs and unmet needs.**

The Law of Opposites

When you experience contrast to what you want, it serves to enhance your clarity about what is important to you and what you truly do want. The truth is, everything you want has its opposite. That is how things are here in our earth school. There is a Law of Opposites. For every up, there is a down. For illness, there is health; for lack, there is prosperity; for loneliness, there is love. The truth is, if you are experiencing lack, you must also have access to abundance. It's the law! Contrast, the opposite of what you want, is your invitation to believe that you will have what you want and to claim it.

It is within your peaceful awareness and acceptance of these opposites that you can be objective and relate to the contrast, not be a victim of the contrast. Only then are you free to emotionally attend to what you want with a passionate intention to receive it. This is how you powerfully attract what you want into your life. Now, let's learn more about how to do just that.

Chapter 13

Acceptance and Forgiveness— The Golden Keys to Your Kingdom

In this chapter I discuss two of the most difficult things to do when you are facing conflict and extremely difficult situations, yet they are MOST important if you want to take charge of your life again. What am I referring to? **Acceptance**

and forgiveness. These *are the two golden keys that give you access to your creative kingdom.*

Acceptance: Let's look at acceptance first. I used to interpret acceptance to mean that I had to tolerate or agree with those things I intended to accept in myself and in others. I had a survival habit of acquiescing to other people's needs. Is it any wonder that I defaulted to this interpretation?

To tolerate was my default setting when I thought I should accept situations I didn't like or accept someone's hurtful behaviors. If you recall from my story, one of my first experiences with acceptance (coping) was when I was a little girl, age 13, in the psychiatrist's office. I was told I had to cope (I interpreted that to mean accept) with the abuse that was happening to me. I profoundly remember vowing that I would never accept what was happening, never. Well, never say never. My non-acceptance wreaked havoc throughout my early adult life.

With profound understanding, I changed my meaning of acceptance: to acknowledge and value another's perspective without judgment and resistance. In other words, to accept means to let go of the fight, to let go of resistance to what is.

Wanting to get rid of your negative beliefs and emotions without first listening to what they have to say about your inner unmet needs only intensifies the conflict between your old beliefs and your new desires. That part of you will get louder if you resist it. It will demand to be heard, accepted, and loved.

Within the process of Alchemy of the Shadow, you will gain a deep understanding of this part of yourself and you will truly be in a place of acceptance. You will understand that your conflicting beliefs are born in fear. Sabotaging as their actions may be, they hold the intention to try to protect you and to bring you love as best they can.

Anyone's fearful or hurtful acts are simply cries for love and acceptance from that little part of them that feels threatened. You don't have to choose to remain in relationship with hurtful people; however, you do need to have compassion for them and appreciate them for the value they offer you. They are mirrors of your own hurtful and rejected selves. When others are difficult for you and they push your buttons, they are really mirroring back to you something you are resisting in yourself. (I understand if that might be hard to hear right now.)

Forgiveness: I first realized that my negative beliefs and feelings were truly on my side when I found myself conversing with my little angry one. I made a choice to forgive my parents. The opposition of anger was felt in every cell of my body as I affirmed my desire to forgive. As I mentioned in my story (Chapter 3), I listened with love to my little angry one as it revealed that its intention was to save and protect me. I realized, for the first time, that I was not my anger. I was separate from it, yet I did have it and it was okay. This information came to me from my subconscious survival pattern, my "fighter twin" who was trying to protect my victim self. It was like a recording that played the same song over and over and over each time I would get triggered.

Because I realized that my powerless, victim beliefs were recordings of old decisions I made as a very young and fearful child, I was able to forgive myself for my ongoing emotional reactions and defensive behaviors that eventually wreaked havoc in my early adult life. My survival patterns certainly did not have the objectivity to realize that I was no longer a child nor a powerless victim. They just compelled me to react by fighting and taking flight.

Survival patterns of beliefs continue to seek resolution of their original intention to save and protect you. They are totally subjective. They are a recording from your past. My profound understanding that some part of me had created my rebellious, angry self to protect me allowed me to be grateful, peaceful, and forgiving with this part of my subconscious mind. I could finally open my heart and accept this aspect of myself that I had shut out and resisted so long ago. I no longer needed my anger to save me from being the victim that I was as a child. I had new information from my higher self. I was no longer a child, and I certainly was not a victim. I accepted that God, the power of unconditional love, was the source of my well-being, not my anger.

Acceptance and Forgiveness Allow for Gratitude and Appreciation

During the five years that I spent in the dark night of my soul, my spiritual quest to connect with a loving God taught me how important forgiveness was if I wanted to feel love and connection with a God who wanted so much more for me than I could see at the time. I thought that forgiving and accepting the negative aspects of myself and others, which included forgiving my parents and the terribly misguided authority figures I had in my life as a child, meant I was choosing to tolerate them or to condone what they had or had not done.

Because of that, I had a difficult time accepting situations and people and forgiving them. Alchemy of the Shadow, which is an ideal method to practice loving forgiveness, was paramount in producing all of the transformations in my life. The experiences I had of miraculously selling my custom homes in 30 days, regardless of the economy and the marketplace, taught me a very valuable lesson in the importance of feeling appreciation for anything and everything, no matter what. You simply cannot feel unforgiveness, with its resentment and negativity, and appreciation at the same time.

When I realized that my negative feelings and fearful subconscious beliefs were not really me, nor were they my enemies, I was able to relate *to* them, not *as* them. Only then was I able to make peace with these aspects of myself and forgive myself. It was in the act of forgiveness that I was released from my past conditioning. It was through acceptance and forgiveness that I truly had the freedom and energy to move easily toward my heart's desires. This is the value in forgiveness. It really is for your benefit.

My initial learning experiences, during my five-year dark night of my soul, required me to give up my attempts to control and to force things to happen. I grew tired of fighting and fearing what I did not want. My inability to accept my circumstances, after I lost everything that I thought I needed to emotionally survive, brought me to my knees and forced me to surrender and to let go.

Resistance Is the Only Thing that Holds You in Bondage to Your Past

When I gave up resisting and I accepted my conditions as being perfect reflections of my inner shadows, voilà! I felt a sense of relief. I had let go of my judgment and resistance to not having what I wanted. It was then that I experienced what I wanted and more, like attracting my soul mate/husband!

This process is easier said than done sometimes. Well, many times. We are so prone to fight or run away from conditions and people we don't want and who threaten us. It is just too scary to let go and believe there is a better way to create the life we want.

If you have been loved and left and perhaps you still feel the sting from that experience—or any hurtful experience, for that matter—forgiving yourself and others might be difficult to accept. You can love your fearful shadow parts of your mind and peacefully release them. Loving them does not mean you are choosing to keep them. It just means you agree to consciously see and expose them and to stop fighting with them or running away from them.

Compassionate exposure and full-body awareness are the keys that unlock the grip that your fear-based patterns have over you. This is a natural process and it releases emotional pain. **Name your emotion without resistance and you can release it.** Alchemy of the Shadow is a process that will help you release your survival patterns of beliefs and their associated emotions. Resistance is the only thing that holds you in bondage to your past conditioning.

Celebrate yourself each time you forgive and let go of your inner resistance to your past conditioning. Celebrate yourself each time you forgive and let go of your resistance to yourself and others, too. Your rich and joyous life depends on it!

It's time to forgive yourself completely!

Alchemy of the Shadow

I have referred to and tantalized you with my miraculous healing process, Alchemy of the Shadow, throughout this book. It's time for you to experience your own alchemy, don't you think? The mere fact that you are still reading "Beyond Your Shadows of Doubt" tells me that you are most definitely ready to have a miracle occur in one or more of these areas of your life.

- ▶ Relationships
- ▶ Money
- ▶ Health
- ▶ Career

These four areas will trigger your survival patterns more than any other. They are so basic to your primary needs, wants, and desires. You no longer have to be a victim of your past or present circumstances. You certainly no longer have to be a victim of your internal resistance to change.

Are you ready to experience what love and acceptance can do for you? You may decide to record the following questions and play them back as a meditation, or you may find that writing in your journal is more beneficial. I find that writing is very effective. It will release your thoughts and feelings onto the paper. You can then go back and discover new insights from your conversation.

Let's do this now. Are you ready? I'm here with you, guiding you along, and sending you love and support as you unlock the door to your creative kingdom!

Alchemy of the Shadow is a process that begins with a conversation between you, your negative feelings, and of course with your very own image of a being that represents power and unconditional love. My loving image was a huge, calm, powerful angel. She was dressed in a long blue flowing, shimmering gown, and it calmed me just to see and feel her presence with me. Did I mention huge, powerful, and beautiful?

So let's begin your "Alchemy of the Shadow" process:

1. State your desire and intention. Ask the negative emotion that opposes this desire to please come forward and talk to you. Promise this little one (your difficult and opposing emotion) that you will accept all that it reveals to you with sincere appreciation. You will very likely feel the resistance as you state your new intent and desire. For example, when I said, "I now forgive my father," I felt my anger vehemently opposing that intention. Use any desire you have.

2. Ask for the name of the little one who does not want you to have what you want. This is most helpful in identifying what emotion needs to be expressed and willingly felt by you. It will reveal the protective intention it holds on your behalf.

3. Calling the little one by name ("little angry one," for example), ask it to reveal how it is protecting you by resisting your desire. What does this little one think it's doing for you? What intent does it hold? How does having your desire threaten the needs and intentions of your little one? You will discover what this emotional part of you really wants and really believes.

4. Listen to this little one compassionately, and value everything it tells you. You will discover the unmet needs that you have been denying yourself. Now thank your little one for trying so hard to bring you love, attention, security, protection, or whatever it reveals to you.

5. Genuinely feel appreciation for that part of you for trying to take care of you. Yes, you may be thinking it is caring for you in a strange way; however, you created this strange way and belief during a confusing, traumatic time in your life when you were very young. Remember, my anger intended to give me the energy to move me to a safer place. I would have been too afraid to move otherwise.

6. Imagine your powerful, loving figure (mine was a huge, beautiful angel) watching over you both as you feel the love between you and your resistant emotion. See brilliant white light surrounding all of you.

7. Have your powerful, unconditional-loving figure give your little one new information. Imagine that your loving power-figure is affirming that you are now consciously aware of the truth of what true power really is and that you have decided to choose love (in my case it was God), as your true source of all well-being, of all that is good and great. Feel your conviction that you have now chosen the power of unconditional love and acceptance to meet your unmet needs.

8. Send a message to your opposing emotion that you now choose love to be your power, not resistance, anger, and resentment. Imagine your powerful, loving figure assuring your little one that you are now being taken care of in a much more loving and powerful way. The intentions of this little one will be satisfied with love, not fear.

9. When you sense a feeling of relief, ask your little one if it is willing to release you. Notice how you feel. Asking this subjective part of you if it is willing to release you, which by its very nature cannot really decide anything different from itself, is really a test of your own trust in yourself and in your commitment to your decision to choose love rather than fear. If you sense, hear, or see the answer is yes, gently release your emotional pattern. See it dissolve into the light and melt away.
10. You are now free to let it go and to focus on your new desire with complete acceptance to receive it. You have entered into your powerful state of choice; you have entered into your creative kingdom!

Congratulations!

There will be no resistance from your feeling pattern toward leaving. You have exposed your fear to the light and you have stopped resisting it. Every part of your being will know that your deepest unmet need will be met in a much better way. Of course, the God energy of love is the best way to do that! No argument there. You will feel convinced that you have truly chosen the power of love over your survival fears to act from and to identify with.

Your Needs Must Be Met with Loving and Wiser Means

If you happen to notice any hesitation from within and you still do not feel convinced that you are free, you can ask your little one what else it needs in order to release you. Maintain your intention to satisfy the essence of what your little one really needs through loving and wiser means. You will feel a sense of assurance and love once you have given yourself permission to have your inner needs met with the power of love and acceptance.

This process will literally shift you from feeling frustrated and resistant to feeling compassionate and understanding. This was the process that lifted me out of the fear-based system I was operating from for the greater part of my early adult life. I increasingly began responding to my life with unconditional love and acceptance. I was free to direct my attention toward what my heart wanted. I had complete permission from all parts of myself to have my heart's desires. I was in my power; my subconscious mind and my conscious desires were aligned. I was beginning to experience the miraculous impact that unconditional love and forgiveness would have on my life.

Experience the miracle that Alchemy of the Shadow provides you!

Your Old Tapes Are Exchanged and Transformed

I have created a guided meditation for you, *Connecting With Spirit*. It is designed to assist you in changing your identity from being associated with your limited, guarded beliefs to an identity as your higher self, your divine soul. This will also assist you in your personal process of Alchemy of the Shadow. You may want to record this meditation in your own voice.

Find a comfortable place to sit and breathe deeply . . . inhale . . . exhale slowly. Relax, and as you flow through these following words with ease, allow yourself, if you can, to feel the sensations that become available to you. Perhaps you will see pictures in your mind; you might experience warm feelings of being understood and valued, or you will just know that someone cares and is willing to hear you in a way you have never been heard before.

> Imagine placing a frame around the following group of words and thinking about what they mean to you: Fight or flight, controlling and judging others, feeling impatient and disgusted, scurrying to be accepted and to fit in, seeking the approval of others, feeling frustrated and angry, and having a deep sense of not being good enough, of being defective or shameful in some way.

Now, looking at this square frame filled with these phrases while keeping in mind your new understanding of what this is all about for you, appreciate how all of this conflict, control, and craziness has been trying to keep you feeling safe, protected, and secure all your life.

Feel their concern for you, like your little pals, trying hard to keep you safe, unharmed, accepted, and secure. Yes, the fighting and anger and the fearful running-away behaviors and attitudes have brought you many trials, conflicts, pain, and poor conditions; however, just feel how hard this group of molded meaningful words, like little characters in a play, has served you. These are all survival character patterns, like recordings that have played over and over and over. You flip the switch on when you get triggered and they compel you to react habitually, without any conscious awareness of the consequences or harm you might bring to yourself and others.

These recordings are totally subjective. They cannot make conscious choices beyond the need to keep you safe. These patterns cannot change any more than a recording can make a choice to change its own melody! Your molded convictions of beliefs that are buried deep within your subconscious mind are like recordings that play over and over and over. They will continue to play until you shut the recording off and play a new one.

Would it not be ludicrous to think that these recordings were going to fight you every time you tried to shut them off? Even more astounding, just notice for a moment that you are looking at these recordings, hearing them, observing them, and sensing them, and realizing how perfectly they have played their songs in your life, exactly as they were programmed and instructed to play so many years ago.

Yes, it is true. You didn't know you were programmed or that you recorded this particular music, if you will. With your new understanding, you feel the excitement and control of being able to shut them off and create new patterns or recordings that make you feel awesome. You are now free to imagine new recordings that can be exchanged for the old ones—new thoughts and feelings that reveal the truth about your greatness and reflect a beautiful love for yourself and for others.

You are sending the old recordings back to the store now, and you're ordering new ones that will allow you to have what you want, new recordings of beautiful and delightful music (emotional beliefs) that will get you where your heart and soul want you to go. You feel confident that these recordings will bring about what you want with a predictability and dependability that the very nature of recordings (emotional beliefs) can offer. And you know it is true because the universal laws and the power of unconditional love of God/universe/source make it so.

See yourself releasing your old character patterns of survival emotions and beliefs, or whatever forms your imagination conjures up. The forms don't matter—only the fact that you see yourself separate from them. Who you are is the one that is observing and choosing what recordings you wish to listen to!

With your new understanding, you can now peacefully accept what a perfect reflection your life has been from the music your recordings have played. Your recordings were magnetic. They drew music into your life that resonated with their original songs. You accepted their melodies as true. They became embedded in your mind because of your intense feelings of certainty and acceptance of them.

The original intentions of your old recordings, which were to help you survive something you feared and didn't think you could handle, have continued to play out in your life experiences. The strategies to accomplish your intentions to be safe, accepted, and loved were detailed intricately and molded exactly in a way that the younger you knew how to best satisfy. You needed to feel better about yourself, to feel more powerful, in control, loved and accepted. And you didn't get what you needed at the time. Now you know, deep within your heart and based on your new understanding and awareness, that's why your life is as it is right now, all of the good and all of the not-so-good.

You now realize that recordings played over and over again are subject to universal laws which bring more thoughts, feelings, actions, and results that harmonize with the original music. It can be no other way—not until you change the recordings, that is. You grow secure in your awareness of spiritual and mental laws—the constant, unchangeable, magnetic force that brings your meaningful intentions into fruition. You now trust that when you consistently and emotionally focus upon anything, the energy of universal power takes shape through your beliefs and feelings. This inner activity must manifest outwardly in your life. As within, so without. It can be no other way! This brings you comfort and security.

You can now accept that spiritual and mental laws are just like gravity. They are a dependable and constant reality on earth. You know you can make choices that cooperate with the gravitational pull of the earth. You do this each time you jump up into the air and you expect to come back down. This is what keeps you from jumping off of high buildings. You see that spiritual and mental laws are no different. They are absolute and unchanging.

With this new understanding, you begin sensing an acceptance of why your life is perfect right now. You relax with the freedom that you can choose not to continue playing these old, outdated recordings any longer. You embrace the freedom that you can create any recordings you feel great about. You can have your unmet needs satisfied with love, and you can experience your heart's desires completely.

The Observer—You

Now you are becoming aware of something quite profound. You might be wondering, "Who am I if I am not these recordings? If I'm not these words and feelings, then who am I?" You might be thinking, "I know I am experiencing the results of these recordings, no question about that; however, it seems I am looking at them, not from the perspective as being them. What is the nature of the me that is looking? All I have ever known is what I've observed my world to be and how I have felt within it."

"Who am I that I am free to exchange the old recordings for new ones that are more loving, accepting, compassionate, and brilliant with joy, new recordings that will draw new experiences into my life that fulfill the intentions of the me that is free?"

Now imagine a color that best represents the nature of this you that is free. Perhaps it is yellow or gold like the sun. Perhaps it is blue like the mighty ocean waves that are roaring with power unyielding to man. Or perhaps it is white, soft and gentle like the winds of spring, powerfully touching the splendor of all the colors in nature. You might be seeing and feeling the passionate reds of the tulips and roses, the deep greens of the leaves, the violets of the iris, and the brilliance and magic of the vastness of the sky. Imagine you are within all these magnificent colors of the rainbow, growing, expanding, getting brighter and brighter, larger and larger, until you feel sensations that are as huge as the sun, now expanding larger than the sun, because you know this energy never stops expanding. It is in a constant state of flow and movement outward.

You feel the freedom unbounded by form, ever-growing outward, increasing, and expanding into the dark regions of unknown space. Floating and bobbing as if you were in a sea of pure, pristine energy, feeling every cell in your body absorbing the energy, you become the energy, free-flowing and peaceful, with nowhere to go, nowhere to be, nothing to do, seeing every cell filling up with light, growing and expanding from yourself until you see every part of you totally filled with light.

And now the light spills over as if a cup were overflowing, continuing to fill up and overflow, moving outward to all the world in love, compassion and acceptance, and total understanding. The real you, your divine soul, is totally permeated with the unconditional love of the God energy that brings life to everything, knows everything from its infinite intelligence, and loves and accepts all beings with total unconditional love, understanding, and grace. It operates through its great laws of the universe, consistent, dependable, and absolute.

Now, from this feeling of vast awareness, if it feels right, accept this truth as your own. Basking for a moment in this freedom, continue seeing the light energy over-flowing from a filled-up you! Yes, you must fill up with this energy before it can spill over. You may have a tendency to give it out before you are filled up. That is okay. Just know you can expand the love within yourself to allow this love and light to fill up inside you, then a natural spilling over can occur.

Love yourself enough to have this love. It constantly flows and will never stop flowing to you, through you, filling up and outward from you to everyone else. That is truly your greatest gift to humanity, your unconditional love and acceptance, the honor and value you now have with your new understanding for all of life. Yes, your conscious mind may choose to participate with certain people, and some it may bless and let go, based on what will harmonize with your truest intentions and desires. It's okay. Be with the stillness of this great energy of unconditional love and acceptance.

You are now feeling safe and secure, knowing you have accessed feelings that harmonize with the all-loving God energy, a pure sense of well-being and appreciation for all of life. The real you never dies. You continue to expand into more of the same all-powerful loving energy. Come to know that this understanding and your feeling of appreciation is aligned with the heavenly kingdom here on earth. Come to know that this is the beginning and the only source of everything in the universe. You can choose to be connected with this divine, infinite love each and every moment, cooperating with it and co-creating for the fulfillment of your truest intentions and desires.

Beginning now from this space of freedom, love, and appreciation, filling up inside, spilling over to others, direct your attention toward that which you truly desire, and know that soon you will experience its outward manifestation, easily and effortlessly.

Jesus said, "Seek ye first the kingdom of heaven, and all things shall be added unto you." (Matthew 6:33) Do you get what Jesus was talking about? Your kingdom of heaven can be experienced while you are here on earth. You can know it by the way you feel and how you subsequently behave; you can know it by the results you achieve. You can know immediately if you are aligned with the truth of your being and with the source of all there is when you feel centered, compassionate, joyful, blissful, grateful, thankful, and appreciative. I would go so far as to say that these higher emotional states of being are heaven on earth.

These higher states of awareness and emotions are available to you in every second, always. When you feel small, inadequate, and powerless, and you experience the emotions that accompany these beliefs, you know you are out of sync with the truth that you are a divine loving soul, made in the image and likeness of your Creator. You are made of the same loving stuff as God/universe/source, whatever name you wish to use.

Isn't it true that a drop of water from the ocean has all of the properties of the ocean? You are like that drop of water. You have the same nature as your source/God. You get to decide how much of the vast ocean of divine love you want to be and to experience in your lifetime.

You've Been Given the Gift of Free Will—Use It Wisely

You were also gifted with your own free will to choose. Divine love and power are always available to you. You get to decide if you want more or less of your divine nature. And this is really good news: I believe it calls you back to the truth when you stray off into your lesser, smaller, fearful self. You will recognize the call through your desires. Life is bountiful, beautiful, loving and joyful when you choose to live from your divine self rather than from your survival characters.

Chapter 16

The Great Shift into Love and Power

s I have mentioned, your negative emotions are a signal that you have not allowed or acknowledged something within yourself or in others peacefully. When you judge, you label people, conditions, and even feelings and beliefs as wrong or bad, and you resist their expression and perspective. Judgments do not let you see other people's perspectives as having

any value. It is a sign that you have closed your heart and closed off the flow of this magnificent energy of love.

In these moments of resisting and devaluing not only yourself, but others as well, you get hijacked from your kingdom of heaven to your shadows of darkness. You return to your fight-or-flight, sympathetic nervous system. **"Heaven" doesn't throw you out; your threatening habits of beliefs and emotions pull you out.** This is why it is so important to stay present and conscious of your feelings and behaviors with yourself and others.

Fighting against the opposite of what you want feels like stress and force. You know this. Remember, contrast shows up as those things you don't want. It is here to bring you more clarity and guidance. You will only experience a push-back if you struggle and resist any aspects of your life that you don't want.

Even the act of ignoring or avoiding someone because you really believe that they will charge into your life and ruin you forevermore will perpetuate your fear. You'll also find this to be true when you fearfully look at or deny your unwanted conditions or negative feelings. This experience can leave you feeling vulnerable, powerless, and insignificant, and you will be unable to feel safe and secure.

Did your checkbook ever improve by you not looking at the truth of its declining, inaccurate balance, fearing it because you felt out of control with your money? I suspect it just got worse, and then your checks could have started bouncing. Maybe you have ignored your blameful feelings about your parents or your spouse or you've hated the conditions of your life. This is the trap I fell into. The financial disaster, which terrified me as if I had been diagnosed with terminal cancer, showed up for me as a reflection of my negative beliefs, my angry, hurt feelings, and my persistent need to avoid facing my inner emotional disaster and my outer difficult circumstances.

Experience a Quantum Leap Back into Your Creative Kingdom!

Now are you getting a sense of how you can and will go in and out of your creative kingdom? You have total control of where you want to be. So you might be thinking, "How do I get back to that beautiful place of love from my 'survival' realm?" This is the million-dollar question that I am going to answer for you now; in fact, I already have. By engaging in the process of Alchemy of the Shadow, you will realize your intention to come back into your creative kingdom, your rich state of freedom, choice, love, and creative power.

The good news is, by unconditionally loving yourself and others and knowing that all people, conditions, and experiences offer value in the greater scheme of things, you will experience a quantum leap back into your kingdom of creative, heavenly states.

If you find it difficult to accept certain people or circumstances, all you have to do is ask for help in seeing the value in them, and you will be answered. I did this with my feelings of anger; I discovered that my anger pattern was designed to protect me and keep me safe. It was in my Alchemy of the Shadow process that I realized all types of expressions are either an expression of fear or an expression of love. Aggression is merely a cry for help to be loved and accepted.

Nonresistance Allows for Higher States of Awareness and Love

I truly believe that when you are willing to let go of your survival system of fear, you will have the capacity to accept different perceptions of other people with compassion, empathy, and unconditional acceptance. This act of nonresistance will flood higher states of awareness and love into your mind/body/life experience, instantly! Love attracts expanded love. It can be no other way. The Law of Attraction is always there to depend on, always.

You can tell when the shift occurs by the way you feel. You will experience a sense of relief when you stop resisting or denying. It's as if the pressure of a closed valve has been relieved once the valve (heart) is opened. It has been! This is the feeling you experience in Alchemy of the Shadow—your resistance and judgments stop and a sense of relief is felt. Acceptance and understanding of "what is" brings relief.

In addition to the relief, you will also feel a strong sense of appreciation, which makes sense when you honestly see the value in all things. You will feel compassion and understanding. Imagine that light and love are pouring through you, flowing outward toward what used to be the objects of your judgments, and now they are the focus of your loving attention.

How can you send out your energy? By focusing your mind on whatever you choose, giving your attention to anything you want with intense feelings of love and appreciation. You may desire a partner, clients, or friends, or, as in my case, buyers for my homes and for a loving husband. Perhaps you would like a material item, such as a new car, your debts paid off, or the cure of a diseased physical or mental condition, to have your physical, emotional, and mental state restored to perfect health.

It's just that simple, yet it is a skill that must be mastered through the practice of loving awareness and forgiveness. I see this as a spiritual practice, and it must be repeated. It is simple, yet it isn't always so easy. Mastering the art of nonresistance makes it much easier and certainly more effective to manifest your heart's desires.

Now, are you getting a sense of the power within this God-force energy and which mental and emotional states will allow it to flow through you? This bears repeating: you are guided by your feelings and emotions as to whether you are in or out of your heavenly creative kingdom, a realm that is permeated with the vast life-giving substance of God—infinite intelligence, all-knowing, omnipresent, abundant, ever-flowing and giving, unconditionally loving and accepting, the source of all there is, both seen and unseen.

The Value and Power of "Desire"

I have identified the value that contrast offers, which is clarity and feedback. I have also described how you "speak" to the universe/God by identifying what you choose to have in your life by giving your complete attention to it—to talk about the outcome you want as if it has already happened, to visualize it in as much sensory detail as possible. My story in Part I described several instances in which I successfully did this.

So how exactly are your desires a part of your growth process? Usually, unless you squelch and ignore your sincere desires, they will be greater than you know how to bring them about. For example, I had a desire for a new car. I had no idea where I was going to get the down payment in the beginning; however, that did not stop me from going for it. I was guided to the right place at the right time and to say the right things to the right people.

Over the years, many people I've worked with to manifest their desires have been reluctant to dream of something greater than their present beliefs would allow. It can be very uncomfortable. They feared being disappointed if their dreams didn't come true, because they didn't have clear ideas on how to fulfill them in the beginning. They realized they had shrunk their dreams to remain comfortable.

Limiting your dreams can give you a sense of security. After all, we humans tend to prefer what is known over uncertainty and doubt. When you do not know how to achieve a desire in its birthing stage, is your typical reaction to reduce your dream or desire and "be reasonable"? If you do, no worries, for you are among the many. Reducing your desires can give you a sense of certainty that you can achieve a result; however, it will be limited and you will fall short of the desires that burn deep within your heart. Nor will you expand and change the limited perceptions that you have about yourself, which I believe is the bigger issue and the greater gift.

What value do these God-given gifts of desire have for your expansion and growth? How can you work with the creative process to bring about a life filled with expanded love for yourself and others, to become free from your past conditioning, and to create the desires you truly want? Let me answer these questions for you now.

The Healing Art Within Manifesting Your Desires

You may originally desire something for the purpose of fulfilling an unmet need from a small part of yourself or as a remedy to get out of your victim state of awareness or ugly circumstances. However, your desires will provide you something very different and certainly much more valuable than what you first imagine. Do you remember my Hawaii story in Chapter 5? I described how I desperately desired to go to Hawaii. I really wanted to feel better about myself and about my world that had come tumbling down around me. I learned a valuable lesson in the healing art of manifesting, and I can best describe it to you this way…

If you have ever been involved in sales or you've been through sales trainings, one of the things you've likely learned is that human beings buy everything for the way it makes us feel. In my numerous sales trainings over the years, I learned how different types of people want to feel after buying certain products. This, I think, is a huge reason we, in our society, are driven to consumerism. Now this is where your new understanding of the value of your desires is going to come into play. You are about to learn the healing art of manifesting.

Think about the car you last purchased. How does it make you feel? Do you own a luxury car and feel unique, very savvy, and successful in the business world? Perhaps you would never buy a foreign car because buying from your homeland feels patriotic and loyal—you feel a strong sense of belonging and you want to support local businesses no matter what. Maybe it is important to make a "smart choice"—a car with great gas mileage that's good for the environment.

Whatever your reasons, if you ask yourself how you must feel after you buy these things, your desired feelings will reveal a lot about your shadow, hidden self, particularly if your desire seems way out of your reach and a bit intimidating. Your desire will feel out of your reach if it is designed to expand your awareness and your sense of self.

Getting Caught in a Sales Trap with Your Desire

Sharp salespeople, either by conscious or unconscious intention, discover early on what we need to feel good about ourselves. They proceed to show us how their products or services will satisfy our [unmet] needs and feelings that we really want to experience. Unfortunately, if we are unaware that what we desire is a remedy to satisfy our deeper, unmet needs, we will be prime targets for their products and services.

We will readily be snared into this trap if their products or services promise to make us feel better about ourselves. We use the material world to overcompensate for what we subconsciously don't believe we deserve to have and to feel. This can be quite costly.

If you get trapped in this snare, you can find yourself spending a lot more money over and over again, rather than working through your inner doubts and fears in the first place.

Unloving, critical patterns of thought (shadow beliefs), as I have been discussing throughout this book, are expressions that do not resonate with the divine soul that you are. If you are intimidated by the way you imagine a new car or a promotion or a trip to Hawaii (as was my case) will make you feel, you will seek after these things in an attempt to make yourself feel better and to prove you are better.

This never-ending struggle to fulfill your deep, unmet needs cannot be satisfied as long as you use the material world to fulfill them. Your unmet needs can only be met through your loving awareness, acceptance of your past conditioning, and your willingness to let it all go in favor of the truth of who you really are.

You may feel better about yourself if you have the "perfect" body, drive that expensive car, or own the big house on the hill; you can have all the trappings of success as I did. However, just as happened for me, when any or all of these things go away, so too will your sense of worthiness and acceptance. You will then find yourself striving to get it all back again.

Your Desires Are Not Remedies for Your Unmet Needs

Regardless of how rich you become, how much recognition you get, or how many beautiful clothes and gems you adorn your body with, these things will only serve you temporarily if you do not become aware of, accept, and transform your shadows—your negative beliefs and feelings. Your shadows will eventually lead you into experiences that will magnify their inner convictions of unworthiness and lack of love. Your inner beliefs will be reflected in your outer world—that's the Law of Attraction.

How do you discover these hidden shadows from your deepest desires? How do your deepest desires serve your process of growth? And how can they become an opportunity that allows more love to flow through you, adding more love to the world? Let me help you understand the language of your desire.

Understanding the Language of Your Desire

Perhaps you feel you are materialistic in wanting more than you barely need. Maybe you feel you will not be spiritual if you allow luxury into your life. Do you judge yourself as being selfish or self-centered if you allow abundance and love into your life? Have you ever had more than you could imagine and then it went away? Well, there's a very good reason for that, and it's not your fault.

What value do your truest desires and visions bring you toward your own personal growth? The answer is revealed in another one of my personal experiences that demonstrates the art of healing within the creative process. Notice where Alchemy of the Shadow integrates into this creative process. . .

The Value and Power of "Desire"

"I'm so tired of this car. It is too small. I don't like the color anymore and it just doesn't feel like what I want to drive. I want a new car!" I decided with great enthusiasm. "This little red convertible has served me well and I have certainly appreciated it, but it doesn't suit my taste anymore."

I began my quest for a new car by writing down what I wanted and when I wanted it. I described how I imagined it would look and how I would feel in having it. I described the car as having soft, pretty, feminine lines, representing wealth and credibility. I was unaware of my longing for these feelings, however. It was in that moment that I realized these qualities of being soft, pretty, and so on, were what I wanted to feel. Wow, all from a car! "What do these things have to do with a car?" I pondered. Then, in a quiet, tender way, I asked myself, "Is there a little part inside of me that doesn't feel pretty, soft, and feminine? Is this car an outward physical symbol that you are speaking to me through?" I asked. "Are you that part of me that is not allowing me to feel these things? I feel your resistance when I try to imagine myself feeling soft, pretty, and feminine."

I then invited the little one who was opposed to me feeling this way to please come forward and talk with me. I surrounded myself with love and light and, as always, promised to love whoever came forward to talk.

"You feel hesitant to allow me to feel pretty," I stated. "What is your name?" I sensed a strong feeling of guilt. "Are you little Ms.

Guilt?" I asked. I saw a picture in my mind's eye of a precious little face nodding yes.

"What is it that threatens you about me feeling pretty and that causes you to resist it? What does Judy being pretty, soft, and feminine mean to you?" I asked.

"I feel guilty when Judy admits she is attractive and desirable," came the reply. "Being attractive and desirable will cause men to do shameful, wrong things to her, like touching her inappropriately," she stated.

"So, little Ms. Guilt, you came alive because of little Judy's conclusion long ago, 'If a man touches me inappropriately, I'm to blame, it's my fault, and I can't say no.'"

"Yeah, it's my fault and I feel so ashamed," this little one replied.

"Oh, that is what little Judy assumed was true. And did little Judy also conclude that if she was desirable and pretty, it would cause men to touch her inappropriately, so she had to be very careful not to attract attention?" I queried.

"Yeah, and I feel so guilty and ashamed because I want attention," she replied.

"Did little Judy feel pretty before she concluded that what happened to her was her fault?" I asked.

"Yeah, she really did, but then it all stopped. She decided never to let herself feel or see herself as desirable ever again. She had to keep from feeling guilt and shame."

I felt immense compassion for this little part of me that had been reaching out to be loved for so long. And through the idea of a pretty car, molded with soft, rounded lines, she has come to

The Value and Power of "Desire"

express, "I want to feel pretty and I don't! I'm too afraid. Please love me and bring me out of my darkness of shame and into the acceptance of light!"

"You think the behaviors of others are your responsibility, don't you?" I responded. "Please accept this beautiful new information . . . others' behaviors are not your fault. You are not to blame for the thoughts, feelings, and actions of others. That hurtful and shameful time in your past was consumed in darkness and judgment, and now you are blessed with a new understanding and love."

I then sensed a very strong presence of energy. Chills spread throughout my body. I then received this message from my Beautiful Inner Being. I had a vision of her beautiful glow and loving face.

"My dearest Judy, you are the magnificence of beauty and love, like the meadows and fields of flowers. You are free to radiate the beauty of your soul with each and every one you choose, blessing the world with acceptance and understanding, as you have given unto yourself and others." I was deeply touched and profoundly reassured by my Beautiful Inner Being's message to me.

I thanked little Ms. Guilt for trying so hard to protect me all these years. I agreed to let her go and she agreed to release me, for she just wanted me to be okay all along. Certainly the love of God, nestled in the wings of my Beautiful Inner Being, was a much better way to care for me. She agreed.

I was later inspired to write this poem, describing what happened on that glorious, liberating day. Can you sense Alchemy of the Shadow within this poem?

Judy K. Katz

The Voice of the Angels

The shadows of the night feel safe, loved, and caressed.
They are inspired to come forward and talk.
They have much to say and much to feel, as silence has been their way.
Listen—for they speak their limits untold, as their hearts reach out for love.

It is all so perfect, so ordered and arranged.
They are safe and free to transform into
their light and blissful ways,
assisting us toward the desires of our hearts.

Nothing to fear, for we are met with Honor and Love, they say.
We are told truths to negate the lies.
All is well. Choice abounds. Freedom reigns.

They are asked, "Where do you move to? Where were you going?"
"Resume," the angels say. "Continue with your love. Continue with your joy.
Continue with your playfulness that abounds everywhere.
Let your beauty forever radiate the energy of that which gives you life."

For All Is Well. All Is Well.

Judy K. Katz

I spent the next few days visualizing what my new car would look like, truly feeling light and pretty feelings—yes, about me—before I ever bought a new car. I felt free to create this car exactly as I wanted, easily and effortlessly, not for the purpose of making me feel pretty and desirable, but for the purpose of expressing the beauty I felt inside.

I did have the easiest experience buying my new car. It was even better than I had imagined. I breezed through the financing, which could have been a challenge, considering my financial picture from years past. It truly was the most enjoyable, perfectly designed car-buying experience I'd had in a very long time. My guidance system was working exactly right, prompting me to be in the right place at the right time. My greatest gift in this experience was the healing that occurred for me. I released a very old lie about me that had produced unnecessary pain and guilt for so many years. I was now free to shine my light brightly and to be seen!!!

To quote Phillips Brooks, a U.S. Episcopal bishop (1835–1893): "Pray not for the tasks [desires] equal to your powers. Rather, pray for the powers equal to your tasks [desires]. Then the doing [manifesting] of your whole work [desires] shall be no miracle, but YOU shall be the miracle."

[Judy Katz insertions]

Chapter 18

The Art of Detachment

By understanding the language of desire—or simply stated, by discovering the meaning and feeling you associate with your desires—you gain the freedom of choice, rather than desperately having to have those desires. Without detachment, you are never free to play the game of conscious creating. Detachment is essential for you to have the frame of mind that allows the creative energy to flow toward what you want instead of dividing your energies between two opposing intentions—one being your new desire and the other being an unloved, defensive pattern looking after you in a frightful way.

In the story I just told, my desire for the car was designed to help me feel pretty and feminine, while my deeply buried and opposing belief was designed to stop me from feeling desirable and attractive, all in keeping with my buried intention to avoid feeling guilt and shame. Since this intention had such a strong negative experience behind it, I felt strong resistance to my new desire for a car. I had a hidden need to feel pretty and desirable again. Within these two opposing intentions, I could have had a difficult time or perhaps never found a car with the requirements I wanted.

Because I was able to let go of "having to have the car," which would have only attempted to satisfy my deeper unmet need to be desirable and to be seen, I was free to let the car fly right into my life—quickly, easily, and effortlessly. I transformed my hurt from the past and I gave love and acceptance to myself. I felt permission, deep within, to feel good about myself, which was the only way I could truly have my desire.

We are here to be co-creators with God. Isn't that what you have been told? Do not give up your visions and desires that have come to you. They are here to serve you by expanding you into more love and truth, which ultimately overflows from you for the benefit of all. Love yourself and others unconditionally and you will be free to create the playground of your life!

I studied, long ago, about the need for detachment. In the beginning, I interpreted that to mean that I should eliminate my desires for material gain. I tried to find a place within me that was lofty enough not to have these desires. After all, didn't God matter more than having things? I thought I could have either one or the other, God or material things, not both. I came to find that I was very mistaken about this subject of detachment, for the more I told myself I shouldn't want the desires I reluctantly admitted to having, the stronger my desires grew, leaving me with feelings of guilt because of it. As a result of this conflict, I went broke and felt very deprived, for my physical world and financial matters were in shambles.

The Truth About Detachment

- ▶ Detachment is not meant to release your dreams and desires, but to release your attempt to satisfy your unmet, unloved emotional needs from the material world.
- ▶ Detachment does not mean to give up on your desires and your vision. It means to let go of not accepting yourself as you are. Using your desires, like your favorite, symbolic goodies— a title or promotion, a designer wardrobe, or the status and lifestyle you think you must maintain, to help you improve your self-image of not being good enough will only increase your attachment to your desires.
- ▶ Detachment requires you to stop fighting against what you're experiencing in the moment, especially when your experience is the opposite of what you're wanting.
- ▶ Detachment means that you give up your non-acceptance of certain people that you distrust and do not like, that you let

go of seeing them as having no value and casting them out of your heart in judgment.

Focus on what you want to create in your life, including others who are in harmony with your desires. Expand what you want from a feeling of love and acceptance. That is the only way that lasting fulfillment can ever be attained.

To consciously create and manifest your dreams occurs from within an emotional frame of mind that blends with the creative energy of the universe. You know this by how you feel. You must have your conscious and subconscious attention on what you choose to have in your life. Shifting into a higher perspective of what is possible and bringing your subconscious mind into alignment with your source energy of love seems to me to be the soul work of our time.

It seems simple enough, and yet masters are few and far between. Be patient as you notice yourself reacting to life from your primordial system of fight or flight, your basic reactive self. You will never again be unaware of reacting from your old patterns of fear. Your awareness will eventually bring you to a place of freedom and choice.

The Mirror in Your World

Your world is so enchanted. People, places and things, conditions you find yourself in, and the desires you feel you want, all lead to one beautiful place. You are coming to discover who you really are—a divine, soulful spirit having a human experience. You are not the negative beliefs that you subconsciously hold to be true, so convincingly true that you forget to question if you have a choice of any other possibilities.

You are coming to know that the substance of everything is the unconditional love and power of God. The energy of God/universe/source is unbounded love and unconditional acceptance. This is what breathes life into all that you choose—more accurately stated, all that you give your complete attention to, particularly with feeling and conviction. This power of God operates through its laws of being, such as the Law of Attraction and the Law of Cause and Effect.

Signs appear in every situation and in every interaction with others that offer you feedback of your internal beliefs and your emotional habit patterns. For example, say you have a job in which you continually feel agitated by your boss or co-workers. Now, in your fight-or-flight response, what would your initial reaction and assumption be? Perhaps your mind would come up with a multitude of reasons why you should be angry at his or her actions, irritated by requests to do menial tasks or by belittling remarks. You find the irritation grows more each day, with added reasons to back up your judgment of this individual. Now, you ask, how can this be of value to me?

Upon a gentle, loving conversation with your little angry one, you may find, beneath all your anger, that there is a little unworthy one hiding in the shadows while being protected by the angry one. In other words, you have an angry fighter charging into certain situations to protect your fearful little one who is in flight or hiding. (This is the symbiotic relationship I mentioned in Chapter 12.) Why would a part of you be in hiding? Perhaps if you were hurt in the past, you formed an idea of yourself that you were unworthy or powerless, that you couldn't speak up for yourself or be successful. You feared you would be rejected or shot down if you did speak up. You could not stand up for yourself without anger coming to your rescue.

Try not to let your intellect decide whether or not this is true for you. Your intellect cannot know what is buried deep within your subconscious. It can, however, look into your world and assess what is happening to you. Your perceptions will be your clue as to what is operating within your hidden beliefs about yourself and others.

When I was a young adult, I observed situations that gave me reasons to believe that women were not valued in the business world by men. I was primed to believe this because I already believed that men didn't respect women, based on my past.

Of course, the more I tried to prove to myself and others that I was a rare exception and different from other women, the more my opposing belief reared its little head to remind me of what I really believed. My angry one compelled me to become an aggressive, successful businesswoman. I needed to hide the fact that I felt unworthy and insignificant, as if I didn't matter. I kept the fight going by remaining angry and resentful, trying to prove I was good enough and worthy to be accepted.

I could never really prove to myself that I was one of the rare exceptions to my belief, and that men would respect me, trust me, and look up to me as a successful businesswoman. I dismissed any evidence that they did. Of course, because of my resistance, my "unworthy self" crashed and eventually brought me to my great fall. This deepened my conviction even further.

Granted, some men acted like jerks. However, why was I in the same experiences with them, feeling so horrible and defensive? The Law of Attraction . . . it's always working, it's always dependable.

Now, how can you use my example for your benefit?

Your world mirrors your inner beliefs, feelings, habits, and survival patterns of fear. It also mirrors the loving and caring human being that you are. Beautiful people and wonderful circumstances are just as much a reflection of your inner world as your shadows are. If, however, your outer world has upset you and your fear and anger buttons have been pushed, this is your clue it is time to go within and do your alchemy work.

- ▶ First, you must be honest about your perception of what is happening in your world. Take responsibility for the fact that your feelings are a response to what **you are subconsciously** thinking, not to what is actually happening. You ultimately have total control of your thoughts about any situation and the meaning you attach to it. You must first become aware of the deeper meaning that is attached to the facts of your situation.
- ▶ Once you are aware of the deeper subconscious meaning about what is happening to you and why, you must step back and breathe. Do not judge yourself. At this point, you can appreciate the fact that your outer world has mirrored back something to you that you need to be aware of which is no longer serving

The Mirror in Your World

you. Your upsetting circumstance or person has provided you the opportunity to do your inner alchemy work.

- Perhaps now you can love that part of you that concluded long ago that you were unworthy and unlovable, or you're not good enough, or you don't matter, whatever the core negative belief pattern reveals to you.
- Your mind may take you to a time (mine often does) when you made that decision about yourself or others. You will understand and see how you reached your negative conclusions. Your subconscious mind had to accept your conclusions as true. It has subsequently played out these truths in your life ever since! Thus, you have attracted someone or something into your life that is a reflection of your inner fearful habits and beliefs.
- Remind yourself that you no longer need your anger to empower you as a means of protection or as an attempt to make you good enough to be loved or to matter. You now rely on the power of love. This is where you can go back to the Alchemy of the Shadow process (Chapter 14) if you are having trouble letting go of your negative, yet justified feelings and behaviors. Call in your angel, your light, whatever image you have used that serves as your power and creative resource to help you.

If you continue with your blame and anger, you will only perpetuate your subconscious beliefs. Do you recall in earlier chapters, I described what happens when you vigilantly and fearfully watch the "tigers" in your life? You get more tigers!

The Law of Attraction is always working, bringing you more of what you give your dominant attention to, consciously and subconsciously. You will either feed your fight-or-flight habits of survival or you'll choose to connect with your heavenly state on earth. Whichever state of mind you choose to feed will grow. It will always be a choice and it will always bring like-kind results: You reap what you sow.

By letting your feelings talk to you (your feelings hold your beliefs), you will discover what messages are being sent out into the universe from your inner convictions, your beliefs. These magnetic messages from your deep inner beliefs and feelings will connect and align you with others who will participate and bring about like-kind experiences that will validate your beliefs.

By making peace with your beliefs and emotions, your little ones, and by giving yourself permission to lovingly satisfy your unmet needs, you will allow yourself to feel safe and release these protective patterns. You will feel relief as your beliefs dissolve in the pristine light of nonjudgmental awareness. This is your magical leap into your heavenly kingdom.

Yes, in that instant of switching from deeming yourself unworthy or lacking in some way, to unconditionally loving yourself—voilà! You will ascend back home. You'll be nestled in the womb of the very substance of love that created you. This is the God-presence, the all that is, and you know it by how you feel—loving, understanding, compassionate, and appreciative. Feeling an unending flow of well-being and joy in a rich state of fulfillment—this is the heaven-on-earth emotional state of divine creative power and love.

The mirror or reflection principle in the universe is another way to see the silver lining in your cloud of seemingly dark, unwanted circumstances. What does your subconscious hold true? Look around with your inner eyes wide open and your heart ready to receive. Then let any unloving person or condition that pushes your buttons show you what needs to be released inside of you. They, or your unwanted circumstances, are a reflection of your inner conflicts and fears.

Choose to have experiences that you truly want. End your conflict within and you will be free to attend to your desires with all your heart, mind, and soul. Your desires will surely be yours in perfect time. Trust that the Law of Attraction is always working, always there! You can depend on it, consistently.

You decide what will be brought into your experience. God/source/universe will decide how. The vision of your new desire will speak to you from the place of fulfillment and guide you easily along. Stay present in each moment and listen for the clues. Stay in love with your vision and trust in the flow of this magical heavenly kingdom state within you.

It was after I completed one of my journaling experiences that I was inspired to write this poem.

Judy K. Katz

An Enchanted World (My Journal of Truth)

I have now filled the pages of this beautiful book,
with the truths untold for so long.
My angel of light with her smile and kind face
met me there as I knocked at love's door—Grant me grace.

I have journeyed from my anger to understanding and peace,
and from shame to acceptance and love.
From my fears to arms open wide just for me,
for the angel of love is acceptance of thee;
This acceptance transformed and set little me free.

For the little shadows of me can come forward to talk.
They are not what is power inside—
They are words I had formed in the darkness of night
as the magnet of thoughts brought their form into life.
For I scrambled the words—brought new form into mind
through my eyes came the power of God.

It is in this enchanted world we live
that speaks so clear and profound;
For who are these shadows coming forward to talk?
Look around—just look around.
The signs are among you, they whisper their name;

The Mirror in Your World

for the magnets of air expand more of the same.
Fear not your enchanted world that's alive;
For it's meant to bring messages from deep, deep inside.

We're here to help, your world resounds, just love us now,
for your power of God will be freed and unbound.
Free to move on to your next beautiful dream—
the one that was locked up inside; now the power of God has been told
—this is it! Be Alive—Be Alive.

Judy K. Katz

Fight or Flight or Your
CREATIVE KINGDOM
—It's Your Choice.

*I*n this chapter, I go deeper into each of these two systems for a simple look into the nature of each and the result that you can expect from each system. I believe the entanglements, problems, and your inabilities to manifest what you truly desire in your heart is an inner system solution, not an outer condition to be fixed. This is why ordinary people can do extraordinary things. Anything is possible because of the inherent power you have from the source of everything in the universe, your personal creative kingdom.

When you operate from within your sympathetic nervous system (your reactive fight/flight/freeze survival brain), you are compelled to do whatever it takes to get safe and to be accepted so you won't be left alone and die. That's what this region is for, to keep you from "dying."

The "Basement" of Your Mind

Your fight/flight/freeze system is like being in the basement of a house. Imagine literally being in a basement. It is dark and scary and it doesn't have any natural light or fresh air. Nothing at all can grow down there. You can't do much in this dark and scary place other than try to keep safe. Your imagination runs wild with all the horrible things that could happen to you. Just remember, this is a place that you get pulled down into when you perceive you are being threatened; it's not who you are! Please never forget that when you feel small, wrong, and not good enough, you're just in the "basement" of your mind; it's not who you are.

When you're in the basement (your fight-or-flight system), you will be compelled to impulsively *react* to the negative behaviors of yourself and others, as well as to your less-than-desirable circumstances from a fearful, resistant state of being. You will feel like a powerless victim and you'll look for ways to survive. Your reactions will be solely to get rid of, run away from, deny, or to try to change what you don't want in yourself and others, and you'll need to do that urgently!

You will harshly judge things and people, including yourself, as being wrong. You might think, "Oh no, no, this can't or shouldn't be!" or "I'm going to ignore this person or problem because I can't deal with them or with my troubling circumstances," or "They are wrong, and I'm not going to speak to them because I'm angry. They deserve to be punished."

Ascending to the "Sundeck" of Your Mind

Now, let's ascend into your creative kingdom. See this like being at the top of your sundeck, just to carry through with my house metaphor that I love so much. You have a long, broad view of your landscape. There is so much light and you have fresh air to take in. You can see so clearly and for great distances. You feel free and unencumbered by anything. You can see and handle it all! You are open and enthusiastic about what your future holds and the adventures you can see yourself taking.

You approach negative people or what you thought were cumbersome circumstances, and yes, even your defensive, attacking behavioral patterns, from a state of centeredness. You feel free to accept what is and to respond appropriately to all situations in ways that honor all perspectives. You allow all of your emotions to be expressed in safe ways that do not bring harm to yourself or others. You have the ability to look for deep hurts and unmet, essential needs in yourself, and you will see them in others as well. You know that your hurts and unmet needs are at the center of all your defensive or aggressive behaviors.

Your work is to [ask] "knock" when your [heart] "door" is shut. In other words, when you notice or feel yourself resisting, judging, and condemning, you know you are in the basement. Ask for love to flood into your heart. Your door will open into your magnificent creative kingdom of healing power and love. It is through the blending of your human nature with your divine spiritual nature that you can create your miracles and desires. Miracles and greatness do not happen through the omission of any of your human or spiritual aspects of your total self. Inclusion is the key to accessing your creative kingdom.

By being willing to approach all things in your life from a stance of cooperation and unity rather than fighting against what you think is "wrong," you will transform your energies and ascend out of your basement and onto your sundeck, your creative kingdom of all possibilities, freedom, love, and joy. By ascending out of your basement and rising up to your sundeck, you will naturally approach your life **without resistance.** This, in turn, will allow life to change for you! Please make special note of that. This is when life will really change for you!

So remember, when you are down on yourself and you really believe you are lacking whatever you think it takes to have miraculous experiences in your life, or to just simply have what you want, it's a system choice that will bring lasting changes into your life, changes that will give you a feeling of fulfillment, richness, and joy.

Change the system you are operating from (your basement or sundeck) and you will change your orientation and perspective toward everything. When you change this, everything will change for you! I promise. That is exactly what happened for me and for the many hundreds of clients I have taught this to for over two decades. Never forget that you are glorious, powerful, and magnificent, regardless of which system you find yourself in.

The good news is that you now have a method through Alchemy of the Shadow to shift from your basement, fight-or-flight system, into your most effective, clear, powerful and loving sundeck, your creative-kingdom system. Condition yourself to practice using my Alchemy of the Shadow process until it feels so natural that you do it automatically. Yes, it's worth it. You will experience a world filled with your dreams and desires!

I believe, from my personal experience and from my extensive studies in how to work with and impact the subconscious mind, that the power of metaphors and symbolism assists our subconscious minds to accept and apply new information in our daily lives. Only then can we truly expect to create a different result. The following imagery is designed to help you do just that. You may find this metaphor helpful to recall as you begin your journey into a new world each and every day of your life.

Imagine that you are a performer in a circus. You have been performing with the lions, tigers, elephants, and monkeys in the center ring and you have become quite skilled at your stunts with these animals. Some you have tamed, others you have trained. As with the lions and tigers, however, your survival has depended upon the use of certain objects to defend yourself should they get out of control. You may have used a whip, a chair, or a large stick. You have grown to depend on these objects and have come to value your sense of safety and control with them. You must remain on guard with these animals, as that is just what they are: wild lions and tigers.

One day you decide you would like to attempt something new. You have been intrigued with the high-wire artists for quite some time. The gracefulness and ease with which they dance across the wire speaks to a part of you that wants to rise high above the crowd and master this art. You imagine feeling light as a feather, walking on air, balanced, sure and calm. This is quite the opposite of the on-guard stance you have maintained with your beautiful wild animals in the center ring.

You begin to learn how to master the art of tightrope-walking. The first step is to learn the fundamental rules of balance and concentration. You are now ready to begin practicing what you have learned. Since this is new for you, a safety net is placed beneath a wire that is not far from the ground. If you should fall, you know you will be protected and won't be hurt. This allows you to concentrate on the task at hand rather than the safety of your body.

You discover something interesting about yourself as you face the wire for the first time. Your body trembles with fear, and your mind tells you to reach for the chair that protected you from the lions and tigers in the past. Your instructor tells you, however, that the use of the chair will throw you off balance. You are reminded that you must balance yourself with your arms extended and free. You are reluctant to let go of your chair; it is familiar and it has always helped you in the past. You try to walk with your chair; however, you are thrown off balance and fall.

After repeated attempts to try to force this approach to work, you give up. You decide to trust what you have learned and realize there is a safety net below. You must keep the wire low to the ground so you will not get hurt trying something new. After much practice, you become more confident, and as you do, you feel secure with the wire being lifted higher off the ground. Eventually, the net is removed. You no longer have a need for it, as you have mastered your new skill.

Facing your fears, letting go of your old survival patterns, and taking on a new way of being can be unnerving at first, just as it was for my circus performer. As in this story, if you are ready to rise out of your fight/flight/freeze reactive patterns when your buttons get pushed by people or events, the old ways of being will throw you off balance and you will fall down into your basement. What you have needed in your basement to protect yourself from your "lions and tigers" will not be effective at all if you want to expand and grow into your higher conscious awareness of yourself and live from your authentic way of being, like walking on the high wire.

You must stay balanced on your high wire. All the protective armor that worked for you in your basement will knock you off balance on your sundeck. You need to have your hands free, to be flexible in your movements, and to be unencumbered by the weight of added stuff to protect you, such as impressive material possessions that never seem to be enough to help you feel better about yourself, a justified self-image that isn't authentic and true, façades and cover-ups galore, the weight that comes from the victim perspective of powerlessness and blame.

You have a choice, and now you are aware it is a choice. Alchemy of the Shadow brings you freedom to choose again. Fear not your shadows. They are the energy of that which, when transformed, allows your dreams to come true.

Just as alchemists turn base metal into gold, you can turn your shadows into your dreams, your fears into love. Reach for the stars; your dreams will always bring you their secrets of fulfillment. Listen to the language of your desires, for they speak of your shadows that are waiting to be loved.

For as is stated in the great book of all time, "Where there is no vision, the people perish: but he that keepeth the law, happy is he" (Proverbs 29:18).

Epilogue

It's time for me to reveal something that I could never have told you before. Allow me to fast-forward into the future to today, 2013. I originally wrote this book in 1995. Yes, it has been sitting on the shelf for almost twenty years, waiting for me to release it. In fact, I wasn't really sure I would ever release it. I worried that this information would not be readily accepted, and I let that belief hold me back. Quite convenient for my shadows of fear, don't you think?

And then my Beautiful Inner Being prodded me, inspired me, and sent me a very strong message that this book must get in the hands of many women and men, and now is the time. So what else could I say but, "Okay!" Now, it is time for you to hear the rest of the story.

For the past twenty-one years, my soul mate, Arny, and I have been happily married. We have five grandchildren, which consist of two sets of twins and a teenage boy. You remember my daughter, Lori. She is happily married and has twin girls, and Arny's daughter, Brenda, is happily married and has three boys: the twins and her teenage son. It gets better. Arny's ex-wife and I are close friends. We have vacationed together; in fact, Jane and I went to Costa Rica last year with her son's future mother-in-law for a women's retreat.

We have been blessed to have all of our family so close that our holidays and birthdays are always a joyous party time! We have had years of laughter, and certainly there have been times of tears, yet always so much love. Love and forgiveness have continued to heal my wounds of past conditioning. Yes, Alchemy of the Shadow is still working inside of me each time I decide to rise up and beyond where I am, and to expand and grow.

If I hadn't had the courage to heal, to discover who I really am, and to embrace all of my human-divine nature, I wouldn't have enjoyed the rich experiences I have had with my mom and dad over the years. Fortunately, as of this writing, they are healthy and they are still with us, and I have a loving relationship with each of them.

The truth is, I had to expand and grow to be able to allow this book to be in your hands right now. I have attained the emotional capacity that has allowed me to let you into my soul's journey for the purpose of helping you to expand into your greater self, as I have done, and as I continue to do.

I've successfully worked with hundreds of women, men, and corporate business owners and their employees since 1997, doing what I love and what I am passionate about in my coaching and training company, Wealth Transformations Success Systems. I've had the privilege to make a beneficial difference in people's lives, both personally and professionally. I've worked with clients all over the world. It is beautiful to realize that no matter where we live in the world, our fears and concerns, our desires to be happy, to be connected and loved, and to know who we really are have no boundaries.

My greatest wish is for you to be inspired by my story of transformation, for you to know that all possibilities are available to you right now, regardless of your past conditioning or present circumstances. You are truly a divine expression of all that is good, which I call God. Please choose a word that fits with your heart; just feel its truth for you. There is no experience in your life that cannot be overcome and transcended. My bottom-line message is this: What you resist will persist. Let go of your resistance to anything and everything and you will experience your personal kingdom of heaven on earth. You do not need fixing, because you are not broken; you just need a nonresistant environment within you that allows your brilliant, authentic self to emerge. This is who you naturally are! My greatest intention is for you to be able to experience yourself through the eyes of unconditional love and acceptance. This is why I have written this book and shared my transformational journey with you, to show you how you too can have a transformational experience and to realize your dreams and desires just as I have.

You can have a rich, soulful, passionate, loving, prosperous, and fulfilled life; it is completely within your reach. It is easier now than ever! There are so many of us on this path to higher consciousness, living from our authentic loving powerful selves, today. We are all paving the way for each other and for those to come, to experience a world that is living from the sundeck rather than the basement. I declare that the dreary, dark times in the basement are coming to an end. It is in our power to make this so, regardless of what current events suggest. Our current events that reek of fear and anger are the effects of the resistance and unconsciousness from the basement.

Please join me and the tens of thousands of other fellow spiritual seekers of truth to live up to your fullest potential, to embrace your divine spirit who is having a human experience. It is time to wake up; your desires are calling you to rise and to transcend your fearful and conditional beliefs about yourself and your world. Please reach for the greater truth of who you are. Feel this calling in your heart and let it guide you accordingly. Your life that you came here to live depends on it.

Perhaps this last poem, which I was inspired to write at the beginning of this book's journey back in 1995, will inspire you at your soul level and lift you up into the bright and glorious light from your sundeck.

Epilogue

A Song from the Angels

*In the shadows of the night when I was born
as darkness and judgment surrounds;
all love, all hope, all acceptance of me vanished and cast me out.*

*The cold and frightened little me could not hold her head up high; for the
weight of the shame and scornful ways sucked all of my energy dry.*

*Be out, they cried, begone, for our shame is reflected so,
and knowing not what is wrong, we feel the weight in our hearts so low.
As all love leaves and heaviness reigns, casting out is all we know;
for we, too, are in dark shadows, and sadly we do not know.*

*And then the flame of light ignites, as that is meant to be,
for the angel of truth awaits each word, to release the truest me!
I am brought to the place in my memory that holds arms open wide to receive,
for it was from this home I was cast out, that did only the damage of me.*

*I have only to open the door with love, as it never is locked or barred;
for an open door to love, I'm told, bathes me in the womb of God.
It is in this womb where all is well and love expands to thee;
that deep and true desires are met and blessed as a gift for free!*

Judy K. Katz

For all I did was to knock on the door,
filled with the weight and shame in my heart,
and the angel of truth then met me there,
revealing the design of my soul, in part.

The intentions I held so high and so bold have now been fulfilled and released;
"You are freed and loved as you always were. Now go and play with the stars."
For the words of humility vanished like magic into light;
I remembered I am love. I held my head up most high.
I now walk with my bounce. I sing with my smile, and
I bless all the world around me;
For I remember the truth as the angels have said, and
I play with the stars found within me.

Judy K. Katz

Recommended Resources

Books:

Awakening in Time: The Journey from Codependence to Co-Creation, Jacquelyn Small (Eupsychian Press, 2001)

Breaking the Habit of Being Yourself, Dr. Joe Dispenza (Hay House, 2013)

Care of the Soul: A Guide for Cultivating Depth and Sacredness in Everyday Life, Thomas Moore (HarperPerennial, 1994)

Daring Greatly, Brené Brown (Gotham, 2012)

Embodying Spirit, Jacquelyn Small (HarperCollins, 1994)

Excuse Me, Your Life Is Waiting, Lynn Grabhorn (Hampton Roads Publishing, 2003)

I Am, Howard Falco (Tarcher, 2010)

The Dynamic Laws of Prosperity, Catherine Ponder (BN Publishing, 2011)

The Power of Now, Eckhart Tolle (New World Library, 2004)

The Seat of the Soul, Gary Zukav (Fireside/Simon & Schuster, 1990)

The Untethered Soul, Michael Singer (New Harbinger Publications/Noetic Books, 2007)

Transformers: The Artists of Self-Creation Jacquelyn Small (Devorss & Co., 1994)

Additional Resources by the Author, Judy K. Katz:

Audios: available at http://www.beyondyourshadowsofdoubt.com
Connecting with Spirit, a guided meditation by Judy K. Katz

Guidebooks: available at http://www.wealthtransformations.com
Roadmap to Emotional Freedom Guide, a complimentary e-book, by Judy K. Katz
Make it REAL: Turn Your Unbelievable Dreams into Believable REALities, Now! by Judy K. Katz

Coaching and Training Programs:

Judy K. Katz offers training and coaching to individuals and groups to accelerate their spiritual connection, attract what they truly want, and release their past emotional conditioning that triggers the fight/flight/freeze reactions and behaviors that sabotage their heart's desires.

To find out more, please contact judy@judykkatz.com.

Judy K. Katz works with organizations, small businesses, and entrepreneurs to eliminate their key relationship conflicts that sabotage success, growth, happiness, and prosperity. To find out more about working with Judy to resolve and transform business conflicts and challenges, contact her at judy@judykkatz.com.

Speaking Engagements for Your Conference Or Event:

Contact: judy@judykkatz.com

Special Bonus Offer

I am deeply grateful for the opportunity to make a beneficial difference in your life. As my way of thanking you for purchasing, reading, and sharing this book, I created an MP3 audio download of the guided meditation, *Connecting With Spirit*, from Chapter 15. This MP3 download is available at no cost when you register your book by going to www.beyondyourshadowsofdoubt.com.

You will need to have a copy of the book with you at the time of registration. You will be instructed on how to obtain the registration code from the book to gain immediate access to the **MP3** audio download.

I trust this will add to your experience in *Connecting With Spirit*!

Blessings and love,

Judy K. Katz

About the Author

Judy K. Katz is an ICF Master Certified Coach and a Certified Spiritual Practitioner. She has been serving individuals and companies for over twenty years to transform the conflicted, resistant environments in which people work and live, from the inside out.

Her passion and specialty is to release people from their inner conflicts and automatic fight/flight/freeze reactions that overtake them in times of critical change, adversities, conflicts within significant relationships, and the everyday relationship stress that results from past conditioning.

Judy is an international transformational coach, speaker, trainer, and author. Her personal journey into her five-year "dark night of the soul" transformed her life completely. This experience brought about miraculous changes in every aspect of her life. She is dedicated to helping others release their debilitating resistance to their human fears and resentments, and to realize the miracles that come from taking back control of their lives. Her students and clients realize their dreams and desires just as she has done in the past and continues to do today.

Judy's mission is to change the reactive way people live and work from the victim's perspective of powerlessness, scarcity, limitation, and fear into their divine birthright of peace and freedom, power, joy, passion, and abundance.

She lives in Albuquerque, New Mexico, with her husband, Arny, and their two Westies, Karlye and Susie. She has twin granddaughters from her daughter, Lori, and one grandson and twin boys from Arny's daughter, Brenda. Judy's oldest daughter, Sheri, and Arny's son, Jason, make the best auntie and uncle ever!

Judy loves and lives for the rich family experiences that her personal transformation has afforded her.

Find out more about Judy's products, trainings, and coaching programs at judy@judykkatz.com

www.ingramcontent.com/pod-product-compliance
Lightning Source LLC
Chambersburg PA
CBHW061300110426
42742CB00012BA/1997